PRAISE FOR THE POTTER'S WAY

'An honest and redemptive story about the power of fun and creativity – I've always said if it was mandatory to wear a smock once a week and get messy with clay, adults would be happier.'
– MIRANDA HART

'This book is a journey, with a map. Like all maps, it relays history, from the first point of contact to pivotal moments along the way. I like a map. They help us to find our way.'
– INDIA HICKS

'A brilliant and inspiriting book about finding fulfilment and serenity on a journey from Prozac to pottery, by the talented Florence St. George, whose every creation I covet.'
– JEMIMA KHAN

'Warm, honest and full of inspiring tips, Florence's story shows us that pottery has the power to soothe the heart and heal the mind.'
– JULIA SAMUEL

T0349337

'Solace and soul-connection via the joy of making. We can all take inspiration from Florence St. George and discover the mood-changing comfort of creativity via ceramics – her way. Or your way. Just do it.'

– LAURA BAILEY

'I am in awe of Florence's story – depression, brain science, pottery, techniques, glazes, artists – she has thrown them on the writer's wheel, and produced this seamless work of art. A truly lovely book '

– MARY THOMSPON

'Written from the heart, this book is absolute proof that working with clay can be tremendously therapeutic. Florence shares her valuable experiences and insights in this delightful book.'

– LYNNE SOUTER-ANDERSON

'I have found nothing outside myself that can truly fill the void, but this book demonstrates that pottery is about as close as it gets.'

– NICK LOVE

'An inspiring story of the therapeutic benefits of immersing oneself in pottery.'

– KATE WALSH

Florence St. George

The
Potter's
Way

A journey of self-discovery and
healing through clay

First published in Great Britain in 2023 by Short Books,
an imprint of Octopus Publishing Group Ltd
Carmelite House
50 Victoria Embankment
London EC4Y 0DZ
www.octopusbooks.co.uk

An Hachette UK Company
www.hachette.co.uk

This paperback edition published in 2024

ISBN 978-1-78072-602-1

A CIP catalogue record for this book is available from the British
Library.

Printed and bound in the United Kingdom

10 9 8 7 6 5 4 3 2 1

This FSC® label means that materials used for the product have
been responsibly sourced

Henry, Iris and Jimmy – if you are reading this at some point in the future, know that pottery is my something and you are my everything.

CONTENTS

INTRODUCTION

Sometimes it's the little things that get you through the big stuff. As soon as the Covid lockdown was lifted, I couldn't wait to visit friends and family again. But I was anxious, too. It had been ages since we'd gone anywhere, and the thought of the journey was pretty nerve-wracking. So I kept a tiny lump of clay tucked away in my bag. I'd popped it into one of those orange Kinder egg cases – my children Iris and Jimmy love these – and stashed it in a side pocket, in case I felt panicky. It's my minuscule stress ball for difficult situations, which nobody else needs to know about, but is always on hand if I need it.

These days I'm better at reacting to my own anxiety – I have a kind of early warning system, which I listen to carefully. I watch out for depression too and as soon as I feel it getting a grip, I take action. This is a book about depression, creativity and the healing power of clay. In my case, it was postnatal depression (PND) – which hit me out of the blue after the birth of our daughter, Iris. Like many women, I couldn't open up and acknowledge that I was finding it hard to cope. Many new mothers struggle to say they're not fine, for fear of bursting the bubble that is perfect motherhood. I never thought for one moment that I'd experience depression – so when it did hit me, I battled on in silence. I wish I could have allowed myself to be vulnerable and express this inner turmoil, but that's so easy to say in hindsight. When you're in it, you often don't realise you're in it, and you're terrified; a rabbit caught in the headlights but with a baby in your hands. If this book achieves one thing, I hope it helps other people to find the strength to admit they're not coping and find ways to get better.

Prozac was part of the solution for me. As Iris grew and flourished and I felt stronger, I began looking for different ways to keep well. Yoga and running have always been part of my routine but there was still a gap that I didn't know how to fill. I love reading, so I naturally turned to books to get ideas. It was from memoirs and self-help guides that I realised that what I needed was a hobby (yes, a proper, old-fashioned pastime). It's not my favourite word, but I read it to mean I needed something just for me other than being a mother to keep me sane. Of course, I struggled with that idea too. For some strange reason, mums often don't think it's right to have 'me time', yet they absolutely crave it and they definitely need it. All I can say is that, in my case at least, if I don't get my own space, there's a high possibility the kids could send me ever-so-slightly bonkers. So, grab that time – it's not only vital for you, it's necessary for the wellbeing of your family.

Thanks to my parents, a creative gene runs through my blood – dad appreciates art and mum makes it – and something drew me towards pottery. I had started watching *The Great Pottery Throw Down* when Iris had gone down to sleep. When the *Throw Down* series ended, I decided to try out a few classes, and I think I knew pretty much instantly that this was the 'something' that I'd needed. Little did I know then that I would end up being a *Throw Down* contestant one day and that this easy-going competition would actually hold the key to my own mental wellbeing, steering me on the course to true happiness.

The good news for anyone who has suffered from depression, or for whom some aspect of life has pushed them over the edge, is that we can rewire our brains to be happier and healthier by doing something that keeps our hands busy and engages our minds too. It was hell going through PND, but I am fortunate that I have a supportive family and the means to access help – basically, my family would have thrown everything they could at making me well again. Actually the answer was something as simple as clay – and you can't get much more down to earth and universal than clay. Gravity is pulling us all towards the mud below – and it doesn't matter who you are, we all get stuck sometimes. Fortunately, I found that mud has the power to heal. My hands are happy when they're playing with clay and my mind is calmer – it's as simple as that.

Except it wasn't as straightforward as that – nothing ever is – because just as I was beginning to discover pottery as a busy young mum, I was a lucky enough to fall pregnant again, with our beautiful son Jimmy. And then, when Jimmy was two weeks old, he became seriously ill and was hospitalised due to the childhood lung infection bronchiolitis. It was easily the worst period of my life, and looking back I can acknowledge that Prozac helped to get me through again. But by this time, working with clay was beginning to bring a whole new sense of balance to my routine.

By the time Jimmy was a toddler, shaping a ball of clay was all it took to bring me down to earth. It has never failed me since. Some of those first pots I made on the wheel made me feel so proud and happy. The 'whoosh' effect of holding something you have made in your hands is powerful, and it most certainly helped me to heal and gave me the confidence to come off Prozac.

Healing is ongoing. Sometimes being in control of my depression feels a bit like being an alcoholic who is working on their sobriety. Just as alcohol may feel the easiest route for some, being down is easy for me, because it's an emotion that I understand. Even though it's toxic, it also feels comforting. To an extent, it's almost like I get a kick out of feeling low, so I'm subconsciously drawn to it – if I allow myself to be.

When the noises inside my head take over, or I'm submerged

in a whirlpool of emotions, it would be so easy to relapse, especially now I'm no longer on antidepressants. However, I've learned to take each day as it comes. I'd love to be up to my armpits in slip and making pots every day because I know that would keep me happy. Obviously, that's not always feasible, so I've incorporated making sourdough bread into my routine when I'm away from the studio. I now involve my kids in all the processes of making clay pots, from foraging and firepits to modelling and messing around on the wheel, so that I can keep my hand in as much as possible. Somehow, just being around clay helps to rein in those negative emotions or voices in my head. With time, it gets easier and easier.

Pottery has transformed my life, which is why I want to share my story with you. It hasn't been easy revealing some of the personal stuff but, by being honest, I hope I can help you recognise something in yourself. I'm not a therapist and I certainly don't have all the answers. I am a mum, wife, potter and the chef of the family, and I love being all four more than anything. When I unexpectedly found myself in an abyss, I needed something just for me – a light in the darkness, a yin to my very own yang.

If you suffer from depression or anxiety, I hope this book will give you the nudge you need to seek help. However, this book is also for anyone who perhaps just feels a little lost. The Covid pandemic changed us all and many of us began rethinking our lives. More and more people are getting fitter or exploring art and craft. Maybe this book will turn you on to pottery – that would be brilliant, the pottery community is one of the most supportive and diverse groups of people you could meet. Both in the real world and online, pottery offers so much – there is always a new clay, a different tool and an innovative glaze combination for you to try. There are endless avenues to explore technically, which means that every visit to the studio brings an opportunity for growth, self-exploration and invention.

Pottery offers an escape route from the news too. When war, politics, pandemics, climate change or consumerism all get too much, I head to the studio. Phones and clay don't mix – yippee! As long as my hands are gloriously mucky with clay I can't go near a screen – what a relief not to be scrolling through Instagram for hours on end.

The best thing about pottery is that everyone can do it. When I started out on my pottery journey, I began with some clay that I had bought online and worked with it in the kitchen. Then I found classes in my local area and before I knew it, I was part of a community sharing a studio space. Of course, it's not easy to fit all this in when you have a job or small children. Maybe you're on your own and you don't feel like there is time or the money to give it a go. It may seem totally out of your reach or your pocket now, but don't give up. It's important to find something just for you that occasionally allows you to sidestep being the provider/care giver.

Never forget that kids love clay too, and if it's hard making it happen on your own, then let them join you at the kitchen table making and creating – it gets pretty messy but as long as they're not stuffing their faces with clay, you'll all have a great time. As I said, it's the little things that can get you through. Whatever craft you find, it may start off as a small distraction but it can blossom into a full-on hobby which doesn't have to be expensive.

Which takes me back to that clay stashed in my handbag whenever I'm on the move. As I've discovered, you can take the girl out of the studio but you don't have to leave the clay behind. I say take it with you and see what happens. If I get a teeny bit anxious I root mine out and roll it between my fingers like a lump of warm wax. Usually, the chatter in my head begins to fade away. I might be with the kids at the park, sitting in the dentist's waiting room or just hanging out with my friends having a coffee. It doesn't matter where I am – this simple act helps to calm the inner quakes. And, if I manage to make something half decent out of it – a pretty pendant, mini dice or bead – then I'm pleased with myself too because I love giving these little things away as keepsakes.

So, this is your invitation to pick up a lump of clay and get your hands beautifully, filthy dirty. The writer Pandora Sykes, in her mid-pandemic essay collection *How Do We Know We're*

Doing It Right?, talks about the craze among millennials for eating clean, deep cleansing, clearing the mind and detoxifying. I would suggest wellness could instead include more atavistic pastimes, like stitching, knitting, crocheting or picking up a ball of clay. Hopefully you will discover, as I did, that pottery is a gift that keeps giving.

As you read my story, please look out for my 'Flea Bites' (Flea is my nickname), which break down the lessons I've learned over time and offer tips and ideas for how to work with clay and incorporate it into your life. Every chapter begins with an 'in the moment' passage where I share some of the best or most poignant experiences I've had while working with clay.

I'm no expert on life, but with my family and pottery by my side I'm loving it and learning as I go.

GLOSSARY OF DELICIOUS POTTERY WORDS

Pottery falls into three simple categories: earthenware, stoneware and porcelain.

1. **Earthenware** – pottery that is fired to a porous state or has a porosity of more than 5 per cent. It is fired at a lower temperature than 1200 degrees C and can be made impervious to liquids by applying a glaze. The best example of earthenware is fired terracotta, which is a rich brown colour, though some earthenwares can be white.
2. **Stoneware** – this category covers a wide range of pottery, from very rough to very smooth, which has been fired to a higher temperature, usually above 1200 degrees C, making it vitrified (see below for what this means!). After firing, most stoneware becomes impervious to water even without the use of a glaze. Unglazed grogged stoneware, however, can leave a damp bottom on vases.
3. **Porcelain** – this also fires to a high temperature, making it fully vitrified and translucent when thin. A more difficult clay to use, so not one for absolute beginners.

Agateware or marbling – by kneading two different clay colours together you obtain a marbled effect that mimics agate stone. Agateware originates from the eighteenth century, but the technique of marbling dates back to the first century A D.

Banding wheel – a turntable operated by hand, used for decorating purposes. You will sometimes see patisserie chefs using them to glaze cakes.

Bat – a plaster, plastic, silicone or wooden disc used for throwing pots on or moving the pots without overhandling them. Also useful for drying clay if they are made of plaster.

Bat wash/kiln wash/shelf primer – a refractory material, flint or calcined alumina, brushed onto the kiln shelves. It prevents drops of glaze from sticking to them or the bottom of the kiln. I try to wash the shelves before each firing – it is laborious but worth it to protect the base of the pot and the shelves.

Bisque or bisqueware – pottery that has been fired once but not yet glazed. As it is still porous, glaze can be applied through dipping, pouring or spraying. The glaze is suspended in water and the porosity of the bisque means the pot absorbs the water content, leaving a coating of glaze in powder form on the surface.

Burnishing – a technique in which clay is polished to a beautiful sheen without a glaze, using an implement such as a smooth stone, the back of a spoon or a lightbulb.

Chattering – a rippling effect which is created on the clay's surface when the pot is turned at the leather hard (partially dry) stage. As the tool jumps over the surface it creates a lovely rhythmic effect.

Coiling – building a vessel by rolling out sausage-like rolls of clay and building them upwards, wound like coils of a spring. By placing them around the circumference of the base and gradually increasing the height, you create a pot.

Extruder/pug mill – a machine in which clay or other materials are mixed into a smooth consistency.

Feathering – this one is exactly as you'd expect! Potters use a feather to indent a texture into glazes. It was one of the first objects used for decorating pottery.

Fettling – a process carried out at the leather-hard or dry stage. It involves either trimming or sponging to remove excess clay, rough edges or seams.

Finger combing – similar to sgraffito, but you use your fingers, rather than a tool, to remove freshly applied slip to create decoration. Really satisfying.

Glaze – fundamentally, this is a fused layer of glass on the surface of a pot, which renders it impermeable to liquids. The addition of oxides gives colour, opacity and other decorative effects. Glaze is thus both functional and aesthetic, sealing a pot for use and making it beautiful.

Glaze firing – is the secondary firing, 1160–1300 degrees C, depending on the type of clay, which fuses the clay onto the surface of the pot.

Glaze trailing – the same application process as slip trailing, but only applied at the bisque stage. The lines that are drawn using the glaze-trailing technique move, melt and absorb into the surface. You can use glaze trailing to create amazing designs.

Greenware – pottery that has been shaped into its desired form but not yet fired in the kiln.

Grog/grogging – grog is a grainy, course material that is added to the clay to give it helpful qualities for building, throwing and firing. It is often used to strengthen pots, add texture and reduce the chances of shrinkage and cracks. Grog can be made from certain types of pre-fired materials including ground-up bricks and waste pottery.

Inlaying – a technique whereby you carve into the surface of the clay and add another colour into the carved-out area to create a design.

Kiln – the oven used for firing clay pots either through flame, gas, wood or oil. More usually in urban potteries they use neutral heat (electric).

Leather hard – the stage during the drying process when the clay is no longer pliable and becomes stiff. It is still damp to the touch and if you press your lips against the surface it feels cool.

Lusterware – a type of pottery or porcelain with a metallic glaze that gives the effect of iridescence. I love to add a gold lustre to the edges of my porcelain shell sculptures.

Piercing – this involves piercing holes in the clay's surface for decoration, or for practical purposes, like when making beads.

Pinching – building or moulding the clay by pinching it with your fingers.

Pit firing – where many pots can be packed into large holes in the ground and surrounded with a variety of materials to achieve interesting colours when fired.

Porosity – is the amount of water fired clay can absorb. When clay is fired to between 600 and 1000 degrees C it turns to bisque, the spaces left where the particles have burned away make the bisque very porous – like a sponge.

Press moulding – pressing the clay into a mould (usually plaster) in order to make a specific shape.

Slip – liquid clay or clay particles suspended in water. Its consistency will vary according to use, ranging from thick cream to buttermilk. It can be used to bond pieces of clay together, to decorate and protect pottery or poured into a mould and used to cast objects.

Raku – a Japanese style of pottery and a firing technique first practised during the 1500s. Raku is characterised by the removal of the pottery from the kiln at the peak of the firing, causing it to cool very rapidly. Originally created for tea ceremony crockery.

Scoring – scratching crosshatched lines into the clay where you want to join another piece of clay to it.

Sgraffito – a form of decoration made by scratching through a slip-covered surface to reveal a lower layer of a contrasting clay or colour. You can be as free as a graffiti artist when playing around with sgraffito.

Slabbing – a technique whereby the clay is flattened into thin sheets – often using a rolling pin or a slab roller. It can then be folded, curved and hand-formed to make your desired shape.

Sprigging – a technique used to apply relief decoration to the surface of a vessel. The shapes are made separately and then applied when the pot is leather hard.

Stamping – indenting a design or textures into soft clay by pressing different shaped objects into it.

Terra sigillata – a very refined clay slip (liquid clay) that can have a sheen when applied to bone-dry clay. This is a useful tool for creating a lovely shiny surface when pit firing.

Throwing – the Old English word 'thrawan' (from which the verb 'to throw' comes) also means to twist or turn. It is the process of making a clay vessel on the potter's wheel, bending, twisting and turning the clay through your fingers.

Turning/shaving/trimming – the process of shaving off excess clay from the base of a pot. This is first done to tidy up the freshly made wet pot on the wheel. It is an important secondary step when the pot is semi-dry. By turning the leather-hard vessel upside down and fixing it on the centre of the wheel, you are able to access the lower section. This process gives the pot and its base a consistent thickness and weight.

Vitrification – when the state of the clay physically changes as a result of firing it at a high temperature, 1200 degrees C, making the ceramic impervious to water.

Wax resist – this is a type of decoration that involves applying a coat of glaze, then painting a pattern in wax, and finally applying a second coat of the same or a different glaze. The wax prevents the second glaze from sticking, allowing the painted design to show through.

Wedging – the process of kneading clay to blend evenly and add plasticity, and to remove air bubbles, which can cause explosions in the firing.

This is just a tiny selection of the plethora of beautiful pottery words out there. Definitions for words like marl, muffle and maiolica or lithomarge, levigation and leathering can all be found in *The Potter's Dictionary of Materials and Techniques* by Frank and Janet Hamer – a must-have book for every budding potter.

1

ONE OF THE GANG

'I had a dream of standing at my potter's wheel in a long line of potters... The line stretched back, and back, through time... the dream gave me a sense that working with clay was taking me to a realm of connection; not only with previous generations, but with the earth itself.'

MARJORY ZOET BANKSON, *THE SOULWORK OF CLAY: A HANDS-ON APPROACH TO SPIRITUALITY*

It's difficult to find Chris Bramble's pottery workshop. I say his name over and over in my head as my eyes dart up and down the street looking for it. I've biked here after dropping Iris off at nursery. I whizz along Kilburn High Road and down a few side streets, bypassing the coffee shops, the florists and bakers I would normally go to. I'm making a U-turn in life and I already feel a bit lost.

As I pull off my bicycle helmet I feel clumsy and nervous – actually, I have the same flutters I used to get when I was going back to school. And I'm having serious doubts about myself. Am I overdressed? How will I fit in around here?

Phew, I think I've found the place. I ring the doorbell. No answer. I try again. Silence. So I knock louder. Finally, I start banging.

'The doorbell is bust,' a beaming face appears at the window above and shouts down. 'He's just coming.' A few moments later the blue door swings open and there stands a 6-foot-4 giant – this must be Chris Bramble. 'I'm here for the taster class,' I tell him and he stands back to welcome me in. 'We have a busy studio today,' he says, as cool as can be, 'but I'm sure we can squeeze you in.'

As I follow him up the stairs, the smell of turpentine sends a happy shiver down my spine – it reminds me of when I worked as an artists' model years ago and it feels good to be back somewhere creative. I follow Chris into a long, narrow room. Shelves are stacked with greenware, bisque and glazed pots. There are wheels of every size and shape, tubs sloshing with water and slip, tins filled with tools and jars jammed with glazes. Crammed into the small area to the left there are three kilns – still warm and waiting to be opened.

Somehow there's still space for the rickety array of tables and chairs. And of course potters – all of whom have paused to give me the once over; well, at least that's how it feels. Suddenly I'm terrified. What am I doing here?

Chris sits me down at the table and gives me a board with a lump of clay. I say a few nervous hellos and I get a chorus of welcomes. Then everyone just gets back to their own work at hand. It feels peaceful but purposeful in this room; nobody is talking too much, but I can sense the spirit of community. So I begin wedging the clay under Chris's direction – roll, roll and a push. And then I'm pinching – press, press and smooth. I'm finding my rhythm and it's in tune with the others in the room…

———

Clay is created from earth and water – just two ingredients and you have this miraculous mush that is the basis of every bit of pottery ever made. Since civilisation began humans have collected clay to make earthenware pots for storing and cooking. Very early on the Chinese added kaolin, quartz and other minerals to the process and invented porcelain – or 'china' – the most magnificent being those cobalt-blue and white ceramics made for the emperors of the Ming dynasty. Fast forward to Picasso, whose funky, playful pots with bulging bellies and arms for handles were like an invitation to all potters to experiment, be versatile and just have fun with the medium. Master potters like Bernard Leach were not so sure about Picasso's attempts at ceramics but I'm a big fan.

These days I'm bowled over by anything that has been crafted from clay – whether it's a humble house brick or a teapot built by the late, great, grande dame of British pottery, Lucie Rie. Even comedian and ceramicist Johnny Vegas' one-minute teapot is a marvel. The voluptuous curves of artist Dame Magdalene Odundo's vessels reach inside and touch my heart, while the luminescent wave plates of Freya Bramble-Carter fill me with awe (Freya is Chris's daughter who, soon after that first taster class, became a great pal and later an artistic collaborator).

‹

My own road to making pottery really did start small. I bought little bags of air-dry clay off the internet and made my first pots on a tray sitting in front of the TV. Then, I set up in the kitchen using spoons and various other utensils as my tools. Before I began my journey at Kingsgate Workshops with Chris, when I was pregnant the second time around, I enrolled myself on a short course at Central Saint Martins. This was my first time in a proper pottery studio and it was here that I slowly got used to the processes – I learned how to wedge the clay into shape, I experimented with the tools and soon found my favourites. I observed the shelves of pottery and began to piece together the stages it takes to make ceramics. I also started chatting with some of the other aspiring potters.

Everybody had their own reasons for being there. Some of them were fed up with their jobs and testing the water, trying to find out whether ceramics was their bag. By this time, I was getting serious about pottery so this course felt like a stepping stone to future things. Prozac was still very much part of my everyday life but I recognised that my new hobby was making me feel better too. It wasn't just the act of wedging, moulding and throwing clay that was healing me. Being out of the house was good too. I began to really look forward to the classes – I couldn't wait for my husband Henry to come home so I could nip off. Clay had captured me but so had that connection I felt with those other students. We'd all committed to the course so that brought us a kind of togetherness. Although it was more than that – listening to other people's stories helped me to forget my own pain; watching them at work taught me lots and brought me confidence.

The Canadian psychologist and TED talker Susan Pinker has drawn on her own studies to present some fascinating ideas about human relationships and how they impact on our mental and physical health. She compared brain scans of two groups of volunteers: the first engaged in face-to-face contact and the second watching videos of other people talking, and discovered that the people who were interacting in the flesh showed more activity in the areas of their brains involved with social intelligence and emotional reward. 'It's a biological imperative to know we belong,' she states in an interview with the *Washington Post*. 'Building in-person interactions into our cities, into our workplaces, into our agendas, bolsters our immune system, sends positive hormones surging through our bloodstream and brain and helps us live longer. I call this building your village, and building it is a matter of life or death.'[1]

I have experienced that surge of positivity for myself on countless occasions. Back in those early days at St. Martins, I remember often feeling tired as I entered the pottery studio, but then I would lose myself in the pots and being around the other students. The hours flew and by the time we were packing up I would feel energised and inspired. As I looked around, I could see the same uplift in the eyes of the others. Louise Ogden, who runs Kiln, a studio in Bristol, describes a similar experience, adding that the time spent away from our phones is another key benefit: 'It's such an antidote to the technological onslaught that has become the norm. It's a very odd thing, clay. People often say they feel like they've been in a spa for a full day.'[2]

When I started researching depression, a piece of advice that came up all the time was to socialise with people. It's for good reason that the NHS makes 'connect with other people' the first of its five steps to mental wellbeing. In her book, *This Too Shall Pass*, the psychotherapist Julia Samuel advocates relationships – which include new friendships – as the first thing to address in her 'eight pillars of strength' for anyone going through grief, loss or change. Both Julia and the NHS recommend learning new skills or finding ways of expressing yourself.[3] If you've found something that makes both these things happen at the same time, you must be onto something good – so two big ticks for pottery classes!

For my mother Sophie, one of the great things to have come out of lockdown has been her connection with her art group. They gave themselves one new project every session – something simple like a charcoal drawing or a collage – but it was enough for them just to be checking in on each other and staying in touch. Sometimes I overheard their conversations, which regularly strayed away from drawings and art and became about what was going on in their lives instead. This is exactly what happens in a pottery class, and it's these lovely little detours, where the conversation veers off course, that can add to that contented feeling that you can get when you're around clay.

If you sign up for pottery classes, you're instantly going to meet a new community and you may go on to make some fabulous friends. Presenter and radio DJ Sara Cox (who presented the first series of *The Great Pottery Throw Down* from 2015 to 2018 – the one that first got me hooked on pots) does a great job of telling the story of a group of women who attend a pottery class at a local community centre in her novel *Thrown*.[4] Characters with various heartaches and problems are 'thrown' together in the class, where they learn as much about themselves as they do about making a pot. I'm not saying that it'll be quite the same for you, but I guarantee you'll enjoy tuning into other people's lives as you sit there moulding your clay.

Of course, you may feel shy the first time you set foot in a class. Perhaps you've never done pottery before. Maybe you haven't done anything artistic since you were at school. The likelihood is that everyone else in the room feels a bit nervous too – we're all grown-ups, but life has a way of making us feel like hiding, whether we're eight or eighty. Once you get your mitts on the mud, though, hopefully any insecurities will slowly melt away – I know they did for me.

Evidently, pottery is having the same effect on a lot of people because there's been a revival in interest across the country. During lockdown, many of us felt lonely but also drawn to have a go at something creative. In 2021, the British Crafts Council reported a marked upturn in crafting and attendance at all kinds of workshops, including pottery. *The Great Pottery Throw Down* has inspired many wannabe potters, partly because the people on the show – the judges and competitors – are down to earth and seem approachable. Some reality shows feel contrived, with the contestants willing to do anything to grab our attention and win the prize. *The Great Pottery Throw Down* is gentler and you find yourself riding the highs and lows with the contestants, willing them to do better and enjoying the triumphs as they happen – plus there is no trophy or cash prize, just the buzz of winning. You get the same feeling in a real pottery class and it can become addictive.

⚜

Huge things happened to me at that taster session at Chris Bramble's studio. When I told Chris my ambition was to make big pots, he and the rest of the class did an amused eye roll. As I now know, it's the classic bumptious beginner's mistake. However, it was as a result of this faux pas that Chris's daughter Freya became my mentor. 'This one's for you,' Chris said to Freya jokingly later that day, implying that she was tasked with helping from now on. Chris was generous to me on those studio visits, and his awe-inspiring work has remained an inspiration. 'What do you want from this in the long run?' he asked me. I immediately felt driven to prove to him that I was serious about pottery. I signed up for weekly classes and made sure I was there consistently. I paid up on time and always did my bit to clean up; where there is clay there is mess. A sign of a good studio that has a tight community is when everyone pulls their weight. Chris is an incredible multi-tasker so I watched and learned how he juggled the different processes. I worked out that there are four areas in the studio; throwing/making/building, drying, firing and glazing. You can easily flit from one area to another; maybe loading and unpacking the kiln while you wait for a layer of glaze to dry. If you think you're done, there's always some good old tidying-up to do. I promise, you'll never be quite finished because you'll find yourself watching the other potters and absorbing all their individual ways of mastering clay.

❧

I didn't realise how much I needed to feel like part of a community until I was in one. I always thought that I was happy in solitude and, having started out contentedly working with my clay at the kitchen table, I hadn't considered the idea of doing anything else. After hooking up with the Brambles, I discovered just how much I loved being in a communal set-up where I could swap notes and tips and learn from others. I have found the same sense of kindred spirit in every studio I have been part of since. It's been life-changing, enriching and it undoubtedly contributed to my recovery.

Just the other day, I telephoned Kit Andrews (AKA 'the Cornish Potter') a fellow contestant on the *The Great Pottery Throw Down*. He makes smooth burnished pots that swirl with

indefinable colour, an effect he achieves through pit firing and constantly trying out new methods. So Kit is my 'phone-a-friend' when it comes to experimenting with unusual firing techniques. A series of moon-shaped pots that I'd lovingly burnished and coated with terra sigillata were lined up in the sunshine, ready to be fired. The burning question was; how to fire them in the pizza oven we were using that weekend? Kit let me in on a few of his secrets and gave me some handy step-by-step instructions. The same morning, I had a chat with Clare Murdock, another friend from *The Great Pottery Throw Down*, about glazes. I finished the day with a phone call to Freya to discuss our collaboration for an exhibition later in the year. At the time I was living in the Bahamas and had my own studio but I did miss the buzz of a shared space. When I got a bit lonely, I would dust myself off (literally, clay dust gets everywhere) and remind myself that I had this fabulous gang who offer advice, support and genuine friendship. They're scattered around the world but they're all just a phone call away.

Clay has this wonderful way of bringing people together and creating a bond that you can't put into words. Last Christmas, I borrowed an idea from Antony Gormley, the artist best known for his giant cast-iron *Angel of the North*. He arranges clay get-togethers, where he has friends over for dinner and gives them all some clay to play with afterwards. As soon as I heard about these dinners, I knew I wanted to do the same. So one day in December, I invited twelve of my girlfriends over for lunch. After pudding, I presented them all with a ball of clay wrapped up in pink tissue paper. Gormley reckons that his guests usually go quiet at this point but then they just dive in and get on with it. I watched intently as my guests unravelled the clay from the paper to see how they'd react. Some of them got stuck in straight away and made something with complete confidence. Others paused and watched, waiting to take their cue. When they got going, they made the most beautiful things; some Christmas decorations, little trinket pots and spoons. I think we all got something special out of that dinner. It's going to be on the Christmas to-do list every year now.

Children love playing with clay or its distant relatives – play-dough, plasticine or kinetic sand – and adults rekindle that childlike glee if you give them the opportunity. I've seen grown-ups giggle and nearly wet themselves laughing as they conjure up a ginormous phallic clay shape, while I've seen others blown away by the satisfaction of having built their own unexpected creations – the 'Wow, did I really make that?' moment.

I'd love to be a fly on the wall at one of Gormley's clay dinner parties, to see what he inspires his guests to come up with. This idea of working together in groups is something he understands well because he did it years ago, for another of his famous installations, the 'Field' sculptures. He started playing with the concept of making thousands of small terracotta figures in towns around the world – from Porto Velho in Brazil to St. Helens in the UK. To do this he needed a band of volunteers from each local area. The process was always the same; participants were given a board with a lump of clay, a jar of water and a pencil and they were asked to make a sculpture of a person measuring between 8 and 25cm. The instructions were simple; the head and body were to be of similar proportions and they should use the pencil to make the eyes – but apart from that they could make the figure however they wanted. Gormley meant the process to feel meditative and collaboration was important to the theme of the work. Finally, these many thousands of tiny figures were positioned in a room with all their eyes facing forward towards the viewer. Gormley calls these installations his 'call to conscience'. He explained, 'From the beginning, I was trying to make something as direct as possible with clay: the earth. I wanted to work with people and make a work about our collective future and our responsibility for it. I wanted the art to look back at us, its makers (and later its viewers), as if we were responsible.'

All those piercing little eyes say so much, but I was awestruck by how Gormley managed to mobilise so many people and bring communities together to create his legions of figures.

In 2014, on the 100th anniversary of the outbreak of the First World War, artists Paul Cummins and Tom Piper asked members of the armed services to help make the famous poppy installation at the Tower of London. Some 300 artists and people connected to the military were involved in hand building the sea of blood-red ceramic flowers, 888,246 of them to represent the British and colonial fatalities in the war, which poured from the 'Weeping Window' and flooded the moat below.[5]

I hadn't even started my pottery journey the day I went to see the poppies at the Tower, but I remember being moved by the story of how it had all come together. Members of the armed services volunteered to plant the poppies – many of them dedicated a flower to somebody they knew who had lost their life. 'Ceramics are transient and fragile, like we are,' Cummins explained. 'They feel part of our very humanity – societies have always been carbon-dated by their ceramics and pottery.'

Now that I have a great affinity with clay, I understand why Cummins chose this medium – clay is of the earth and the earth unites us all.

FLEA BITES

- Being part of a community, clan or any good old club makes me feel stronger. Depression can feel lonely but I found a safe place with people I trusted and felt more supported. Being part of a community is also about giving back – whether that's teaching or just doing 'yer bit'. I hope it will make you feel good too.

- Freya Bramble-Carter was recently described as 'the goddess of pottery', and I was extremely lucky to become one of her pupils. Hopefully, you'll find the crockery god or goddess of your dreams. There are new pottery studios popping up everywhere as the craft becomes more and more popular with people from all backgrounds – actor Brad Pitt, musician Nick Cave, tennis player Serena Williams and fashion designer Sonia Rykiel are just a few famous apprentices. A quick Google search should bring up local studios. Check out local adult education schools or art colleges for classes too.

- If you can't access a studio and are looking for remote learning, then try organisations like the Ceramic School on Instagram, where they post new, free tutorials every week.

- I found that having low expectations at the beginning really helped. Being open to learning and remembering that all those mistakes that you're bound to make will help you understand the process. Don't presume you can throw big or build something huge in your first class – like I did. It's better to start small and grow.

- If you have 15 minutes to pause in your day – watch artist Ai Weiwei's talk about his *Sunflower Seeds* installation at the Tate Modern from 2011 on YouTube. It's incredibly moving to see how clay brings communities, villages and the artist together.

2

PINCH POTS, PREGNANCY AND POSTNATAL DEPRESSION

'... *Here she is, just a few months old, clear clay to work wonders with. No doubt, if I could, I'd mould her into something wispy and adoring, but fortunately, she'll have none of that. Like any other child, she is a unique reality, already something I cannot touch, with a programme of her own packed away inside her to which she will grow without help from me.*'

LAURIE LEE, *THE FIRSTBORN*

I can feel my little boy kicking and pirouetting inside me... the kicks and the jabs at my ribcage have been getting stronger. Sometimes, if I change position those little flicks feel less intense, so I sit down at the kitchen table. I sip my hot cup of tea and get back to the damp clay in front of me.

Working from home means that I don't have all the tools and moulds that are offered at my current shared space in Kingsgate Workshops, so I've returned to the primitive technique of just pinching the clay. It's a great way of working with very little mess. And just getting into the rhythm of pinching and smoothing the clay helps ease my mood, leading to a calmer day.

When you're manipulating clay, it can feel almost like speaking in another language. Somehow my fingers want to make the same shape and form again and again. I pinch, squeeze and massage these little sculptures and line them up in front of me. Each delicate piece is like a shell and every one of them is just a little larger than the next. So on a whim, I place one 'shell' inside the other and they cradle each other like Russian dolls.

I touch my own belly to find out how my boy is doing. I've been so immersed in making that I'd forgotten about the kicks. He's all quiet for now – perhaps the calm that the clay has brought me has registered with him. He's peaceful and safe within, I picture him growing and thriving inside me.

———

Looking back, I was lucky. Both of my pregnancies went well, but there was a kind of innocent wonder when I was expecting

Iris. I absolutely loved the feeling of that growing bump – I felt in control – what could go wrong? I'd read all the books, scoured the internet and made a birth plan – I couldn't wait to be a mum. At the same time, I was realistic about what lay ahead – baby books had prepared me for broken nights, dirty nappies and even the 'baby blues'. I must have skipped or skim-read the chapters about postnatal depression – I just didn't think that it could happen to me. It wasn't something that was discussed by friends and family. Now I know that one in ten women will experience depression in the year after childbirth, but back then, having depression wasn't on my radar and there was never any sign that I would be the one in ten who got it.

Our beautiful, sunny girl Iris was born on the 22 July 2014 at St. Mary's Hospital in Paddington in London. It was summer. The sounds from the street party wafted up to the room where I was going through a long and painful labour. Coincidentally, Prince George had been born on the Lindo Wing opposite this birthing centre exactly a year before and people were celebrating the anniversary – not that I could because I'd had an epidural and was strapped to every monitoring device going. My high expectations of having the perfect birth were dashed because my baby was back-to-back, which means she was the wrong way round. My husband Henry and my sister Christabel stayed with me while my father Andrew managed to sneak off for some Dutch courage in the local pub, though not before grabbing a few puffs of the gas and air pain relief when the nurse wasn't watching. It all felt fun, exciting and typical of my family, which I loved.

Iris was born at midnight and Henry left the hospital at 1am – we had both agreed that a night on the hospital floor just wasn't worth it for him. Suddenly, I was alone with my baby – well, in a ward with eight other mothers hidden behind curtains and netting – but Iris and I were together in bed and I remember just looking at her. Like most new mothers, I just wanted to cradle her, touch and smell her soft warm skin, hear her tiny sniffles and suckles and feel her gentle breath. She was delicious, my little shrimp. She'd spent nine months growing inside me and now here she was very much alive and making adorable little snuffling noises. Helpless yet strong, a gift from nature, a creation way beyond comprehension – did we really make her?

I was blissed out and in love. Yet, that first night in hospital, somewhere inside my tired body and fuzzy brain, I knew something was not right with me. I didn't feel happy in the way I'd expected. In some ways I felt overly euphoric. Could I be delirious? Was this normal? Something indefinable, a shot of anxiety, had registered on my internal radar, but it was tiny and I hoped it would just go away. I told myself pregnancy hormones are powerful – they are potent chemicals – so it was no wonder I felt a bit strange. Now, I recognise this momentary unease was

the beginning of a depression that would evolve into something much darker. I called Henry the following morning and suggested he come and get us. By 9am we were home.

Well, in one sense I was home – back within our own four walls and in my bed. But it would be many years before I was truly home in my own skin again and I have clay to thank for helping me get there. These days, the panic attacks and anxiety I sometimes experience can be assuaged by playing, pinching or kneading clay. If I tune into how the clay feels, I'm closer to understanding what's going on inside me. Sometimes I wonder whether I would have healed more quickly if clay had been in my life when Iris was born.

⟨

Symptoms of PND can descend like fog on a winter's day. Sudden, brutal and blocking out the sun. Or, they can be gradual, more like snowfall, where each tiny flake adds to the mass and before you know it you're in deep. By the end of the summer, I knew I wasn't right. That niggle in the hospital had mushroomed into full-blown panic. On the day that Iris was born, a Malaysia Airlines plane crashed in the Ukraine. I became convinced and terrified that planes were going to fall out of the sky and kill us. Living in Fulham under the shadow of the flight path to Heathrow was petrifying – every plane that traversed the skies made me shudder inside. Walking down the street became distressing because I was convinced the fumes from the buses were poisoning my baby. I knew these thoughts were irrational so I hid them from my family. I didn't want them to think I was mad and hysterical. But I felt both those things – as well as inadequate, guilty and sad.

Like most new mothers, I was exhausted. There were, of course, the sleepless nights when Iris cried and I felt clueless as to why. I now know that she was hungry, and if I had known it then I would have probably felt even more guilty. In the daytime, there was hardly a moment to grab a sip of tea. If I wanted to exercise, I took the buggy and Iris with me. 'Me time' was a thing of the past. This independent, egocentric young woman, who had been able to whizz about wherever and whenever she wanted, just didn't have a clue. At night, I'd crawl into bed exhausted and tearful but still struggled to sleep. When I did snatch some sleep, my dreams were hot and heavy and I would wake up bone-tired – I felt ill prepared to look after this perfect little creature at my bedside.

By winter, I was getting into regular rages. If somebody had put a ball of clay in front of me then, I'd probably have thrown it at the wall – or at Henry. Poor Henry, he wanted to help me, but I was determined to breastfeed and that was where it was all going wrong. We didn't realise that Iris wasn't latching on correctly. Everything Henry tried to say or do to make it better set me off. If he suggested a bottle, I shouted at him. When he smiled at me, I wanted to scream. Sometimes I just told him to 'fuck off' – even in my sleep (sleep talking recording apps captured these events). I knew all this wasn't right, but I couldn't stop myself.

Why all this rage? I felt so lost and in pain. The mental drain became physical. These were all classic symptoms of PND, but at the time I was bewildered. I heard the murmurs of concern from everyone in the family: 'What is going on with Flea?', 'How long is she going to be like this?' Meanwhile, there was this insane urge to run. In the past, if I couldn't cope with a situation, I would put on my running gear and disappear out the front door. Running released the endorphins that made me feel calm and able to cope with anything. If I had a boyfriend and we were breaking up, then I'd do a runner too rather than talk about it – Flea by name, flee by nature. All my life, running had been my default mechanism. But with Iris, for the first time, I couldn't just up and go.

I take a deep breath in as I write this, aware that Jimmy and Iris may read it one day, and I need them to understand that PND is caused by a chemical imbalance – a shift beyond a mother's control. I hope that in my own quest to understand what happened to me I'll be able to help them when they go through their own hormone changes. I want to be able to talk about it and break the cycle of suffering and silence. If we can open up while we knead and play with clay together then all the better.

Obviously, the maternal side of me never wanted to escape because this perfect creature was my daughter, my responsibility and I loved her. There was, however, this terrified voice telling me to get up and leave. This is a very difficult feeling to explain. I felt so much guilt for even feeling that way. I felt like a terrible mother and a terrible person. I'd been confident that I was going to be a great mother and that I would instinctively know what to do. I wouldn't need a village to raise my child. I would be completely fine. I wasn't.

Christmas was the catalyst for change. Henry took me by the hand, literally and metaphorically, and together we went to seek some professional help. The lull between Christmas and New Year is not the ideal time to see a doctor, but now we'd made the decision, we were keen to get on with it. We made an appointment with my gynaecologist because we didn't know what else to do, and he referred us to a psychiatrist. The night before that dreaded appointment we lay in bed and I cried in Henry's arms for ages. In my younger years, I loved a good cry when things had gone wrong or I was in trouble – it added to the drama (exit stage left and all that). These, though, were painful tears. The kind that leave you gasping for breath. Henry hugged me tight and tried to reassure me.

❧

It's funny how I can remember something so clearly when at the time I felt displaced. Henry and I were in the consulting rooms of Dr. Van Huyssteen in London. It felt like everybody else was still celebrating Christmas but we were sitting in this sterile room, holding hands tightly and praying for an answer.

'What are your hobbies?' the doctor asked gently. My mind went blank. Normally, I would have reeled off tons of interests – putting together photograph albums, embroidery, collecting art, baking, running, yoga... so many things. Right then, in that room, I just couldn't answer him. I had *no* answers – I couldn't think of a single thing I enjoyed anymore.

'What do you like doing?' he prompted. Again, my head was empty. I loved being a mother, I loved being a wife, a sister, a daughter, but I couldn't access the words. I'm lucky to have such a supportive family, but I couldn't express how much I love being with them. All I could feel was emptiness. 'I don't know,' I said, because there were no words in my head and my heart felt numb.

There was this enormous void. Right then there was nothing I liked doing. And it was absolutely terrifying to admit it. Not just for me but for Henry too. My loving, generous and supportive husband was at a loss. He looked nearly as frail, confused and scared as I did. Henry remembers that moment and has since explained how very frightened and worried he was that the loving, carefree young girl he fell in love with was never coming back. And, in his darkest hours, he was asking himself the same questions as I was: 'What the hell is going on?' Of course, this doctor knew straight away and he prescribed Prozac (fluoxetine). There is a range of treatments and support for PND, but my doctor felt my case warranted antidepressants. Some women have access to other routes, including psychological therapy or diet and exercise. Everyone is different, but my healing began that day, when I took my first dose of Prozac. Within a few weeks, the fear and guilt started to fade and I began to climb out

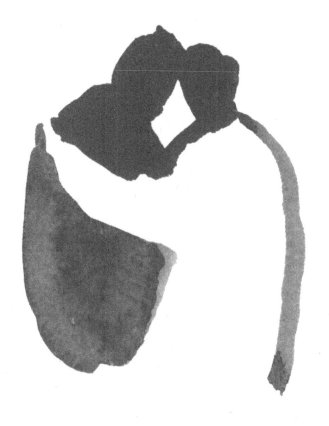

of the deep, dark well and feel like my old self again. I was able to continue enjoying motherhood.

There is a lot that can be said about Prozac and it's definitely not the right treatment for everyone. I believe it was the turning point for me. There were times when it took me higher than I perhaps have ever been in my life and when I got to that place, I felt I could see things more clearly than I ever had. It made me wonder, 'Is this how everybody else feels all the time? If it is, have I been living under a rock my whole life?' It was a breakthrough that allowed me to find myself again. Prozac played its part in helping me to become the mother, wife, daughter, sister and friend that I dearly wanted to be.

Once I started to feel a little in control of my own illness, I wanted to understand it more. I needed to dig deep to discover the causes, delve into my own history and see whether the signs had always been there. Is depression genetic? Does it run in families? Or can we learn ways to reset the button and create a new shift for the next generation?

Of course, lots of factors are involved and we definitely don't know or understand them all yet. Some recent research into PND reveals that it can be genetic, especially the most severe form, postpartum psychosis. I'm grateful I didn't suffer from that, but my illness was frightening and isolating. How did something so black find its way into my life? I had never had cause to think my mum had had PND herself, but after my experience I began to suspect that she had suffered too – she was lucky having four children, but it must also have been hard work. I didn't feel able to wade in and just confront her about it, but the next time she came to stay with me for a few weeks, I made sure there was time and space to talk and offered to show her what I had been writing. Perhaps if I shared my story she might tell me more about what happened to her.

My mother says, 'Love multiplies with every new child; it never divides.' She has always been true to her word, and now she has grandchildren, that pot of love just seems to keep growing like in that fairy tale, *The Magic Porridge Pot*, recounted by The Brothers Grimm. I love mum's saying and truly believe that we humans have this wonderful capacity to love. I feel it myself, not only for my own children but when I become an aunt again or when one of my friends has a beautiful new baby – I get that gush of love and wonder all over again. Our bodies, however, tend to keep the score. We don't grow physically stronger each time we have another child. I know mine feels more tired and frazzled – and that is after just two babies. We don't magically sprout extra pairs of hands. Some days I'd love to have eyes and ears in the back of my head. Mothers are miraculous creatures, but often it gets too much – even for us. How was it for my mum?

We were sitting opposite each other as I read her parts of this chapter as I was writing it. I'm new to writing and didn't realise how often you find yourself adjusting your thoughts as you go. I also didn't know that the very act of writing, particularly about yourself, can sometimes unleash more questions than it provides answers. I was quite nervous and stumbled over the words sometimes, especially when I tried to catch my mum's eye and gauge what she was thinking. I really couldn't work out whether she felt proud or concerned about my vulnerability.

After I'd finished reading, we both reached for the mugs of tea on the table. I was waiting for mum's response and I wondered if she was finding it hard to express whatever it was she was feeling. No wonder her response was dislocated – I think she felt both of our experiences deeply. In fact, mum didn't reveal too much that day; she just gave me a few snippets of what she had gone through. It was enough for me to know that she'd suffered too. She admitted she had felt depressed at times although it was never diagnosed – it rarely was in those days. I felt her pain and loneliness even though it had all happened years ago. We hugged hard. I hope she felt some kind of relief from confiding in me – but just as the door opened, it was shut again. It's a place that she perhaps doesn't want to go, and yet for some reason I do.

Still waters run deep, and I certainly stirred up the mud that day. Just one conversation and there was this new understanding between us – it was a turning point in our relationship. The mud is still settling but everything is clearer. Knowing about mum's difficult moments changes everything. Now I can rake through my past and admit that I wasn't the easiest teenager to grow up with – but I can be gentler on us both because mums and daughters rarely see eye to eye on everything. Even though we still disagree sometimes, I know she respects me as a mother and appreciates how I parent my kids. I'm keen to make sure we continue learning together and sharing experiences, wisdom and creativity.

Another thing is clear: mum is a total survivor. She is a fabulous loving mother but also this fascinating fizz of creative energy. Perhaps this was her own path through depression and somehow gave her the strength to go on without CBT, pills or therapy. She tried a few different things before she found what she loved doing. First there was garden design and later she enrolled at art college, where she finally explored all that pent-up creativity that had been bubbling inside her for years. Since then, she's had exhibitions and solo shows of her prints. She's also written and illustrated her own book of recipes, *Mummy's Chocolate Cake*. I'm so proud of her and happy that she has found the things she loves doing. And I'm grateful knowing that some of her creativity is lurking in my genes – albeit alongside a possible propensity for depression.

Something else I've discovered is how PND can affect our

partners and other family members too. What happens if it's your mother or wife who has the illness? In his memoir *The Scent of Dried Roses,* the author Tim Lott unravels his mother's depression and subsequent suicide.[6] Like me, he was looking for reasons for his own depression and believed that his mother had unwittingly 'given' depression to him. It's so sad how depression can take us down the wrong avenues in our head. Long after her death, Tim was given access to his mother's medical records, and it was only then, when he pieced together the various documents and notes, that he recognised she had been living with PND. Throughout her life, she'd been prescribed a cocktail of s edatives and other tranquillisers but the depressive episodes just kept recurring. When you read stories like Tim's, it becomes even more apparent how important it is to shine a light in the darkest corners, to face up to problems and break the loop. I think that being enlightened about my own 'stuff' has enabled me to build healthier relationships with the people I love, especially my children.

I wonder how many other women suffered in silence like my mother and Tim's. Up until the 1980s, PND wasn't even a recognised medical term in most countries. Before that, if a woman had a 'change of mood' after having a baby, it was most likely to be filed under 'nervous condition' and the episode was labelled 'a nervous breakdown'. Sadly, for many women, the best they could hope for in terms of treatment was electroshock therapy.

I guess if I want to understand why I'm sharing my story with you, I need look no further than my own mother. We can't heal the past, but we can help women in the future by sharing our experiences. If Iris and all our daughters have children of their own one day, I hope they'll be stronger for knowing about what happened to us.

⸎

When I was about six months pregnant with Jimmy, I began to make a series of pinch pots, or rather pinch pots within pinch pots, which now litter my bookshelves all over the house. At the time, I don't remember thinking, 'Ooh, I will make a pot that encapsulates how being a mother makes me feel.' However, in hindsight it's easy to see that motherhood was at the heart of these pots. I was just moving my fingers, pummelling and pressing the clay and unconsciously creating pots within pots that looked like little hatched egg shells. Pots that were so fragile they would often crack and break in the kiln. Now it's easy to see my vulnerability as a young mother-to-be expressed in those delicate walls. My mind was looking forward to our new baby, but my body hadn't forgotten the turmoil it went through after the birth of our first child.

Did you know that clay has a memory too? You will sometimes find that the clay you've been working with pulls back into another shape – as if it has a mind of its own. I once noticed this whilst placing my clay in a mould. When I returned to see how things were going, the clay had curled up at the edges. This was a new phenomenon for me, but it's something that experienced potters know all about. It often happens when the clay has been overworked and somehow remembers a previous shape, which it then tries to recreate. Apparently, the earth's surface has a memory too. When I visited Kenya in 2022, the country was experiencing a devastating drought. Everywhere I looked there were large black cracks scarring the red landscape. Year in and year out, the earth fractures in the same places – new cracks are a rare occurrence. It's another mystery of mud and something that reminds me of how memories twist and shape us too.

As I've ventured further on my pottery journey, I've learned how all my experiences impact upon each other – like tectonic plates moving beneath the surface and affecting the earth on top – so my present is never far away from the past. The potter, therapist and trainer Lynne Souter-Anderson has written about this in *Touching Clay, Touching What? The Use of Clay in Therapy*.[7] Lynne uses clay as therapy for children and adults going through a variety of trauma and anxiety, and often refers to it as a 'medium' because it allows us to bridge the unconscious and the conscious. As she puts it, 'what comes out in the clay is born of us'. She watches her clients carefully when they first make contact with the clay because it's like the beginning of a relationship – with the same whoosh of thoughts and feelings. This first experience can be so powerful that she likens it to a birthing process, 'every client is different and who knows what will be engendered?' When I was moulding my 'mother and child' pots, I had no clue what I was doing, but in retrospect I was playing out my own internal fears about motherhood.

My introduction to clay was through pinching pots and I still love this technique – slabbing, coiling or sculpture are other ways of hand building (as opposed to working at the wheel). These days I tend to have some idea of what I'm going to make when I go to the studio, particularly if I have a commission, but with pinching pots I can go with the flow and let things evolve.

To pinch a pot, you begin with a humble ball of clay and press your thumb in the middle (which is why they're also called thumb pots). Then you roll your thumb around until you've created a kind of well. You can keep on digging, wiggling and smoothing with your fingers or you can begin to pinch and press the clay into shape. There is no right way to do this – some potters start with slabs of clay, rather than balls, and pinch upwards. This is fine, as long as the walls of the pot don't get too thin so that it collapses, at which point you may feel like punching pots.

The more experienced you get, the easier it is to forget to take time to touch, feel and connect with that initial wholesome lump of clay, but it's an important thing to do. By checking in on it, you can check in on yourself. Does it feel cold or warm or perhaps a little dry? Is it soft, smooth and pliable or just hard and uncompromising? What does that make you feel – and, actually, how are you feeling today anyway? It could be a fleeting thought or a barrage of stuff, but listening to yourself is an interesting mind game as you hold that ball of clay in your hand at the beginning of a session. It's like when you sit down at the start of a yoga class and the teacher tells you to 'arrive' on the mat. In her lessons on YouTube, yoga teacher Adriene Mishler talks about setting the intention for the practice. Whether you make it something big or small, it's a great way of tuning in to what's going on in your world and recognising the shift in your feelings from the beginning of your session to the end.

This mindful act always reminds me that I've accomplished something new that day. It also helps me to be honest with how I am feeling. Sometimes I achieve something I didn't know I had in me – and by checking in I can acknowledge this, which feels hugely empowering and gives me confidence in everything else I do. Even if I've had a crap day in the studio, it enables me to review the situation and ask myself, 'Why?' Was I was heavy-handed because I was pissed off about something? Or perhaps my piece was lacklustre because I was simply feeling lousy. Most of the time, though, just being around clay allows me to be a bit easier on myself. Most people know the saying about crying over spilt milk – well there's no reason to cry over cracked pots either. The process of pinching pots has been around since humans began digging in the dirt – it's as old as civilisation itself. There have been enough archaeological finds to show that humans have been creating functional hand-built pots for eating and storing food and drink for thousands of years. Some of those ancient Greek or Roman crocks were pretty sophisticated and many were strong enough to withstand storms, volcano eruptions (Pompeii has a treasure trove of pots) and the rough and tumble of everyday life.

One of the many beauties of pinch pots is their intimacy. Sometimes you can see the fingerprints or finger marks of the artist, imprinted in the clay. That gentle, personal mark is captured for evermore during the firing process – or until the vessel breaks. I do it myself – I create the rippling effect on my sculptures with my fingerprints. Sometimes I see people looking closely, trying to figure out how I did it, and it often surprises them when I explain it's something as simple as my fingerprints…

The contemporary British ceramic artist, feminist and peace activist Elspeth Owen takes this pottery journey one step further by suggesting that people should touch her works, as she believes that it is only through running your hands over the skin of her pots that you can discover their true character and sense their fragility and their strength. It's a process she calls the 'unavoidable knowing'.

Now when I pick up my mother and child pots, I can feel the fear and fragility that I imprinted into the soft clay. I didn't recognise it then, but those feelings about motherhood were captured by the firing process. And once I started looking around, I found there are countless artists, sculptors and potters who have explored the same subject and found parallels in their emotional journey. One such artist is Barbara Hepworth, whose *Mother and Child* (1934) sculpture speaks to me deeply. When I consider that she had five children (including a set of triplets!), I wonder how on earth she managed to combine being a mother with the time-consuming work of chipping and smoothing away great hunks of stone into such tender works of art; abstract yet pulsating with love and emotion.

It's hard enough being a mother or an artist, but Hepworth somehow did both and kept a journal for us to read all these years later. 'I've slowly discovered how to create for 30 mins, cook for 40 mins, create for another 30 & look after children for 50 & so on through the day. It's a sort of miracle to be able to do it – I think the secret lies in not resisting the chores & drudgery & carrying the creative mood within oneself while cooking so that it's unbroken.'[8] I certainly can identify with this feeling.

Sometimes it's difficult to discern if depression came before motherhood or vice versa. I know that clay fills the space inside me, and as it does, it helps to spill the secrets. I don't think I'll ever have all the answers, but as long as I have clay at hand then I'm healing and feeling and getting closer to understanding what my life is about.

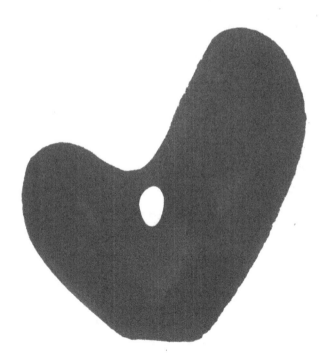

FLEA BITES

- Start small. By making pinch pots or fashioning beads with some air-dry clay, you don't get overwhelmed. Mastering slip casting or the potter's wheel takes practice, but moulding small pieces of clay in your hands is a perfect way to start.

- It's okay to pinch sculptures as well as pots. Look for inspiration in your family pet or reach for a book and pick another animal that you love. This is a great activity to do with children, who are often happy to let their imagination be their guide. Jimmy has a collection of dinosaurs that we pinched and moulded together. We always start with a sausage-sized lump for the body and then pinch out the wings and legs. From there, anything goes – bobbles of clay for eyes and spikes cut out and added along the top. Jimmy cherishes his collection of creatures and I like them because, unlike many toys, they aren't plastic and can be recycled.

- If you need some inspiration, seek out the work of ceramicist Melissa Weiss, who is the queen of pinch pots and sculptures. Her colourful collection of pinched cups with stems was inspired by her granny's Tupperware, while her 'people candle holders' have also been pinched and moulded into existence.

CREATING YOUR TOOLBOX

- As you delve into the world of pottery, you will inevitably collect your own hoard of tools. I bought a bog-standard toolbox in my local DIY shop and started filling it with 'treasure'; instruments for fettling, sprigging and moulding (some of my favourite pottery words – see Glossary).

- Every tool becomes personal to you and you'll soon discover the ones you love. Bamboo tools are fabulous for smoothing two bits of clay together to seal the joints. Ribbon tools come in all different shapes and sizes and are used for the satisfying process of turning and removing ribbons of clay from the surface of the pot. Kidney tools, so called because of their shape, come in metal and plastic and are used for shaping and smoothing. Throwing ribs have a hole in them (so they look just like a Barbara Hepworth sculpture) and are used for throwing pots as well as burnishing and smoothing down.

- Sponges are essential for most processes and you'll need a stash of big, medium and small ones. You can even get them on sticks so that you can delve deep into the belly of your pot to remove water or smooth it down.

- Do you remember that back-to-school feeling when you filled your new pencil case with highlighters, colourful erasers and fresh Sellotape? I enjoy that same feeling when I acquire new tools. At the start I didn't know what half of them were for but I still got a real thrill when I found something different to add to my collection.

- Try experimenting using stones, pebbles, feathers, spoons, biros or other things you already have at home to do specific jobs and see what works for you.

3

MY FERTILE VOID

'Hours can pass without thinking or caring about anything else – that's what is known as the "potter's nod". It's a feeling that's very similar to being at the mercy of a wonderful drug, except in this case, it's a holistic antidepressant.'

JENNIE JIEUN LEE, *VOGUE*

This isn't a race. I've already rolled out my long snakes of clay. They're waiting next to the banding wheel. A pot of slip is standing by. The small disc of clay I fashioned for the base is on the wheel – this is the foundation for my grand design.

Carefully, I begin winding the lengths of clay around the base. A skilled bricklayer knows how to build a wall by carefully setting each brick in just the right place and applying the correct amount of slip 'cement' to glue the brick to the wall. It's not so different when you make a coil pot. The coils must be uniform, and in the right position, before I press them together using the slip. It takes time, concentration and instinct to get it right.

Gently, I scratch and crosshatch the surface of each coil (a process called scoring) before filling the scratches with sticky slip. When the coil feels in the right place, I begin pressing and 'gluing' it to form the walls of the pot. Slowly and surely, my pot begins to take shape. This is when the fun starts to happen and I'm pleased there's time to play.

With my sticky, slippy fingers, I'm pressing the clay and smoothing the walls. But I've gone too far – I've pinched a hole in one of the sides. Do I keep the hole or fill it in? Sometimes a hole can be repaired. The process of hand building is slower than working on a wheel and it allows me to push the boundaries, and play with whatever mistakes I make.

I add a little more slip and, as my hands move up and down, the pot starts to open up like a lily. I watch, letting my hands and the clay do the work in unison, only occasionally allowing my brain to step in if it's starting to look like the Leaning Tower of Pisa.

This pot has taken on a life of its own, but there's no rush. I'll set it aside under a damp rag until tomorrow and then I'll decide which way to go. Maybe I'll close the hole and, who knows, it could be a keeper.

———

I'm often guilty of charging to the finish line. Sometimes, the anticipation of what I might create gets the better of me. Pottery isn't a hop, skip or a jump – I try not to let my excitement get in the way of the process. I just have to slow down and roll with it. Coiling a pot, in particular, stops you from rushing ahead. It's only you, your sticky fingers and the lump of cold clay. There's no need to keep up with the wheel as it turns. Everything is done at your pace.

In my first years as a potter, I used to sit outside in the open air coiling. Being barefoot, listening to the wind in the trees and the birds singing while slowly building my pots, was calming and grounding. It's a shame it didn't always work out: being outdoors has many obvious benefits but too much sun can warp your pot, while a blast of dry wind from a particular angle can make one side dry too quickly. So now I sit half in, half out the studio, with the door open so I can take in my surroundings while I sculpt.

Now, when I look back at those days of being at home with Iris as a toddler, I recognise that a new happier person was beginning to emerge. PND had been an episode in my life, but I didn't want it to define me and I was doing my best to get better. I had found a happy little routine, bath times were filled with giggles not angst, Henry and I were working as a team and I was beginning to find quiet moments in between the six meals a day, endless laundry and nappy changes. I was 30 years old and I was still very much a work in progress – aren't we all, no matter how old we are? I was subconsciously waiting for what was next in my life, while actually being quite busy at the same time.

Some days, I yearned for a bit of freedom – time to have a shower, go for a run or read a book when I wanted to, maybe to meet up with my old friends. I was the first of my crowd to have a baby and it really did put me in a different place. Many of them were busy with their successful new careers or in early stages of relationships. I remember being asked to organise a hen party after a month or two with a newborn and finding it so hard to explain to my best friend that my head just wasn't there. All I could think about was the hours of sleep I was missing out on and if I needed to buy nappies. If I'm honest, I was lonely, and that's a hard thing to admit when you love being a mum. I wanted something else too – another avenue for me to explore.

What was this mystical 'more' that I wanted? I didn't know myself. Exactly what did I want to be? What did I want to do? I didn't know. But I was excited. I didn't feel hollow inside as I did on that dreadful day in the doctor's office. Now I felt optimistic and that something new was on the horizon – I just hadn't yet figured out what.

By this point in my life, I was used to feeling a bit lost when people asked me what I did – often there was an awkward moment and I'd bat them off with a big smile and my favourite line of defence: 'Oh, you know, I'm Jack of all trades and master of jackshit.' The things I had done were a bit random, and didn't make me feel particularly proud. When I was in my late teens, I worked as a fashion model and I was very happy to pack that in – I had quickly grown disillusioned with it. One time I was told off by a fashion photographer as I had a few wisps of light-blonde hair on my thighs – I remember being seventeen and cringing in the bathroom, aware of this chitter-chatter next door, and then a stylist popping her head round the door to suggest I shave the blonde wisps away.

I also tried acting but being in front of the camera was nerve-wracking. There were good times, of course – learning to shimmy with Saif Ali Khan for my role in the Bollywood hit *Love Aaj Kal* in Mumbai was fun, but it didn't make me feel fulfilled. It wasn't the 'thing' for me. It was art that gave me real satisfaction – afternoons spent visiting art galleries and auction houses with my dad, on the lookout for talented new artists. If castings for modelling or acting jobs took me to West London, I'd steal twenty minutes and nip inside the Royal Academy to check out the latest exhibition. For a while I tried my hand at organising art shows, but once I was a mother it became tricky fitting it in.

So what to do? I had always loved making art myself, but somehow I lacked the confidence or stamina to go for it. Often we have voices in our heads that stop us from doing the things we really want to do. The ones in my head were pretty bossy. Added to all this was a chorus of 'You can't do that!' from what seemed like everyone around me: 'Oh your sister is a writer – you can't do that!', 'Ah, your mum is an artist, you could never be as good as her,' or 'Your brother is a sculptor, that's his thing.' Be aware of this chitter-chatter – otherwise known by psychotherapist Julia Samuel as 'the shitty committee' – because it *is* in your head and it can stop you making the right choices for you. Just because there is one artist in the family doesn't mean there isn't room for another...

Looking back on it, I realise I was going through some classic stuff. My depression had been profound but now I had an eighteen-month toddler and I was on the mend. With determination, aided by Prozac, the world had been realigned. To survive, I'd also started structuring my days. Creating a routine that included good habits helped put me back in the driving seat. Actually, part of my routine was down to having Iris – yes, she would wake me up at the crack of dawn, but that encouraged me to start a routine. Luckily, Iris slept well at night so Henry and I had time together. We'd nip out for an evening walk with Iris in the pram and stop by our local pub for a drink. Summer walks, family picnics and ice creams in the park were moments that I still treasure. Life was calm. Finally, I felt like a good mother. It was during these peaceful months of doing nothing very much

that my creativity began to flow. Little did I know then, but I was slap bang in the middle of my very own 'fertile void'.

I first read about the fertile void in the book by Julia Samuel that changed my life, *This Too Shall Pass: Stories of Change, Crisis and Hopeful Beginnings*. It was one of those 'now it all makes sense' moments. You may wonder why I reached for such a book when I wasn't grieving in the traditional way. I guess I was still trying to make sense of everything that had happened, and the book was recommended to me because Julia addresses all kinds of loss and offers some brilliant ways of dealing with depression and change. What she made me realise is that becoming a mother is one of the greatest transitions we make in life and that, even though motherhood is a joyful new beginning, it also means the end of your previous life – being young and care-free, for example – so we do experience a sense of loss and it takes a long time for the emotional self to catch up with the physical self.

After reading Julia's book, I was keen to find out more about the concept of the 'fertile void'. I discovered that it originates from Gestalt therapy,[9] and is taken to be a kind of lull or space in our 'Cycle of Experience' that allows time to discover what is next for us. Perhaps we are in a manageable routine, or just experiencing the calm between one thing and the next. As our energy is not being sucked in any particular direction, our subconscious mind is free to roam and quietly heal itself. Either way, it's an unconscious process but with hindsight I know that's where I was.

Anyone can reach a point in life when they question who they are, and it doesn't necessarily take a great trauma for this to happen. Maybe we are hurtling along at great speed and so evading the answers is easier. Some people keep busy with work or packed social diaries. Others prop themselves up with drink, drugs, sex, food – the list goes on. These coping mechanisms only hold for so long. For some people it comes to a point when they begin to feel like they've lost control or maybe they spiral downwards into depression. It's then, if we can step back from all that distracted us and kept us so busy, that we can discover the truth about ourselves. Rather than charging headlong at hundreds of miles per second, we can pause and open up to new possibilities.

It's an exciting idea and now that I've discovered it, spreading the word feels right. Think of it as a kind of gap year for the soul or a magical mystery tour to a happier you. When I first sat down with a lump of clay, something inside me burst open and I felt alive again. Perhaps pottery will do the same for you, but it could be anything creative – and that's a thrilling prospect.

⌁

Coiling pots is a good way for anyone to start learning about clay because you're not tied to the wheel. There is time to experiment and learn, and discover the properties of this wonder stuff and how it likes to be treated. You need to concentrate as you build the pot, but when you have the basic structure and you begin to smooth the coils into shape, you can really let your mind go. Smoothing clay is wonderfully grounding. It's as soothing as a dummy. At times it can be meditative and allow you to enter a kind of mindless zone. You might find that when your hands are kept entertained, your heart and mind can be too.

Contemporary ceramic artist Dame Magdalene Odundo builds her pieces by hand, creating great sensual pots that evoke the curves of a woman's body. In an interview with *Apollo* in 2019, she described how, in order to capture the essence of what she is trying to say in any piece, her hands have to be in direct communication with her heart.

There is serious science behind this. Pottery has spurred me to explore the connection between my own mental health and brain chemistry and creativity. And the more I discover about these links, the more I believe that art therapy can work for so many people. Clay is 'my something' but I'm sure painting, working with wood, sewing, glassblowing, strumming a mandolin, or doing macrame or anything crafty and creative could give you a whoosh of feel-good neurotransmitters too.

I have touched on how having structure in one's life can be a great way to fight depression. But there are also theories that doing the opposite can be very effective too – that is, jumping out of your comfort zone and doing something that breaks your patterns. When my children were tiny, I read *The Whole-Brain Child* by neuroscientist Dr. Daniel J. Siegel and parenting expert Dr. Tina Payne Bryson, a great introduction to the theory of right brain and left brain. They explain that: 'the basic idea is that while the left brain is logical, linguistic, and literal, the right brain is emotional, nonverbal, experiential, and autobiographical – and it doesn't care at all that these words don't begin with the same letter.'[10]

I've learned that in order for my kids to be happy and fulfilled, both hemispheres of their brain must work together. The same is true for adults, and one of the best ways of achieving this is by doing a hobby that requires you to focus. Plonk me in front of my ancient potter's wheel and I'm beyond focused – I'm in my own world, a warm and happy place where mindfulness and mindlessness meet and creativity flows. I can almost feel the dopamine, endorphins and serotonin kicking in just thinking about it.

Worries about money, climate change and political unrest have a huge impact on mental health for everyone. Antidepressants can be a very good short-term solution – they were for me. These powerful drugs affect our neurochemistry, including production of the hormones adrenaline, cortisol and glucocorticoids, which can trigger depression. But neuroscientists are making new discoveries about our brains all the time. One idea gaining increasing traction at the moment concerns the effect our behaviour can have on our neurochemistry. Something else that fascinates me is how the neural connections in our brain are constantly reconfiguring – the technical term for this is 'neuroplasticity'. Through my research I have learned that there is a possibility that we can rewire our brains and 'programme' ourselves to be happier – by changing the things we do, rather than relying on pills.

Dr. Kelly Lambert is a leading neuroscientist – some call her a 'brain whisperer' – who has been researching this concept for years.[11] She believes there are natural ways to stimulate our brain to combat depression, and this is based on becoming more physical – especially with our hands. Dr. Lambert has carried out studies with rats and humans which show that being engaged in effort-based activities and keeping our fingers busy is great for our brain because it increases our serotonin and oxytocin levels. In the past, women were actually prescribed knitting for anxiety. Diver Tom Daly has talked of how he turned to knitting and crochet to keep himself grounded during the Olympics. The idea of giving someone who is feeling low some knitting needles and a ball of wool may sound far-fetched but it actually makes sense if you apply Dr. Lambert's findings. I'm delighted because it's another giant 'yes' for giving pottery a throw.

The research is demonstrating that there is credibility in my own story of pottery and healing – that centring a ball of clay is a physical manifestation of something that can happen to us inside. Certainly, clay has transported me from a place of nowhere (my fertile void) to a life with endless possibilities...

FLEA BITES

- The fertile void is out there for all of us. I discovered pottery but it could be something else for you. Allow yourself to pause and discover something new.

- Hand building is a slower process than working on the wheel, and encourages you to really slow down. Think about the texture of the clay. If you build up too quickly and the clay is over wet, it will splay out like a dying lily. Give each coil time to dry just a little before you add the next one. You can use a hand dryer or hairdryer to help speed-dry each coil – but be careful not to overdo it because it may get brittle and crack.

- It's a good idea to prepare your coils in advance. Find a dry, clean surface and roll the clay with your palms. Make even-sized snakes of clay by applying a really light, steady pressure. Lay 'the snakes' under a damp tea towel until you are ready to begin building. Some studios have a clay extruder which produces uniform coils of clay.

- Try making your own tealight holders by coiling. Start small and you'll soon find the confidence to make something bigger, like a mug or even a teapot. Be adventurous and bold. Why not make arms for handles and even a nose for the spout on your teapot? Just make sure the spout is hollow, so it pours (I've made that mistake!).

4

THE WHEELS GO ROUND

'The strokes of the hammer on the chisel should be in time with your heartbeat. You breathe easily. The whole of your body is involved. You move around the sculpture, and the whole of you, from the toes up, is concentrated in your left hand, which dictates the creation…'

BARBARA HEPWORTH, QUOTED IN *BARBARA HEPWORTH: ART & LIFE*

My feet are grounded on either side of my rusty old wheel. The foot pedal of this wheel is now so stiff and covered in rust that I use the handbrake to accelerate and stop.

I throw the well-kneaded ball of clay against the wooden bat and it lands with a satisfying thud. The simple act of throwing mud onto a hard surface feels amazing. I breathe out and release a little of what's been holding me back today.

When you are starting out, centring your ball of clay is the trickiest part of throwing a pot on the wheel. I remember when I was learning, it often felt like neither my hands nor my feet would obey me. The wild wobble at the wheel would often go from bad to worse until the clay would catapult across the room, flying off the wheel like a frisbee. These days I feel in charge. Instinctively, I get into position – my feet are firmly on the floor, I tuck my elbows into my body to anchor my arms and my hands glide over the spinning clay, shaping it up into a cone and down again until all is aligned into the centre. My head engages too. Somehow, I know the right moment to make my move.

℃

Now it's happening – I can still feel a gentle heartbeat drumming rhythmically through my body and into the clay. When I am in the moment like this, I feel connected to it. I lean against the clay – hard enough for it to listen to me, but soft enough so that it doesn't feel tortured. After years of yoga practice and painful hand injuries, I've learned to keep my back straight and use my core muscles to centre the clay, rather than push against my wrists. Mind and body work together to create the balanced strength I need to ground myself.

And then suddenly, there it is – a beautiful, centred ball of clay. It's taken practice to get here but now it feels so natural and it can happen so quickly. I'm sitting here in quiet wonder – where shall I go today?

———

Centring the clay on the wheel is one of the first steps in creating a beautiful uniform pot, vase, mug, jug, egg cup, sake set or soap dish. It could even be a paddling pool for a fairy garden (an invention completed with my sidekick, Iris), a Venus Flea Trap sculpture or another 'out-there' project. Whatever it is, it must be centred and so must I be – focused and on the ball. Some of my dream-pieces have slipped and died a spectacular death on my wheel, drooping and dripping with water. Others have mushroomed out of control because my hands lost the plot for a second while my mind was trying to catch up with the wheel as it whizzed round. Sometimes, I've just let go at the wrong moment, or I've pushed too far, and my creation has gone off-centre and flopped before my very eyes – and yes, I've yelped in pain and experienced a little heartache when that's happened. These days, though, I'm mostly relaxed about things going wrong – I just squish the clay into a ball because I know it can be recycled and I can start all over again.

There are several steps to master before getting the centring of your pot right. It all kicks off with kneading or wedging, which blends the clay if you are using two separate batches. It also increases plasticity and, most importantly, ensures there are no air bubbles that could cause explosions in the kiln during firing. It's a step that shouldn't be skipped or rushed, which proved very tricky for me. My comfort zone was what the French call '*vite et mal*' translating as 'quickly and badly' (something that was often written in my school reports). I've learned to slow it right down even in the early stages of kneading and wedging.

Once you get into pottery, you may well find it exciting to watch other potters in action. Once, over a two-week Christmas holiday when I couldn't go to my studio, I strayed onto Instagram (and shhhh, even TikTok), and before I knew it, I was scrolling endlessly through pottery videos. Instead of feeling FOMO (fear of missing out), now my scrolling had purpose; I was learning, picking up tips, forensically analysing different styles. Sometimes, the temptation even got too much at night and I'd end up in bed on my phone watching more potters at play.

Florian Gadsby is a potter I find hugely inspiring, with his precision and ingenuity. He works totally on his own, so must be well organised to make and film the way he does. He cleans up, prepares and processes the clay and creates these amazing sensory videos, filled with satisfying thuds of clay, swishes of slip and the hum of the wheel. There is so much to learn from him and he shares his skill so generously on Instagram.

Adam Field is another favourite Instagram potter of mine. In his timelapse videos, he makes the creation of his bold coil pots look effortless. I get buzzy just watching him pull off big hunks of clay, using his hands and tools to bash and smooth it into submission. Sometimes, it's good to break a few of your own rules and get hooked on social media. My excuse is that with pottery, you'll never stop being curious for new tricks – I bet even Lucie Rie was!

Michael Cardew was the first pupil of potter Bernard Leach. Cardew went on to become one of the most influential ceramicists of his day, and his slip-decorated earthenware is highly collectable. He taught pottery in Africa before returning to teach in the UK, and when you look at his slip-layered, sgrafitto'ed pots you can really trace that African influence. Recently, I've been trying my hand at making big earthy Cardew-style pots, so I sought him out on the internet. His primary teaching method was by example, so it's a total joy to watch crackly old footage of him in his studio as he talks you through what he does. He was doing this long before any Instagrammer but you can root him out on YouTube. One film I watched was made when he was in his eighties – I can only imagine how many tons of clay those great gnarly hands had kneaded and turned into pots by then. Yet there he was rolling his sleeves up and getting back to basics, extolling the need to knead and showing how to do it properly by swinging your body and using your whole weight, because, in his words, 'If you use your arms you'll get tired.' He calls it a mechanical skill – something like swimming – which he learned in two weeks by doing it every day for five minutes before breakfast. It stayed with him forever. I'm with Cardew on this; wedging is a skill you'll never forget, but to keep doing it as long as he did, you need to remember your arms are an extension of the core. When I say core, I mean those muscles around the pelvis and lower spine. Remember to engage your core and you're set for life.

Most people start with ox or ram's head wedging. Again, there are lots of tutorials online but basically you start with a lump of clay shaped like a brick. Once it's in front of you, you position your hands on either side of it, with your palms on the top and fingers wrapped around the sides. Next, you push the clay down and away from your body, digging your palms into the clay so that a raised mass remains in the centre – if you squint it looks a bit like an ox/ram's head, hence the name. My best advice is not to push too hard and, as Michael Cardew says, use the weight of your body rather than the force of your wrists and hands. This technique is deeply satisfying when you get the hang of it. The motion of rolling is calming and soothing.

If you want to take things to the next level, and fancy a bit of a workout, give spiral wedging a go. This technique can produce a sort of childlike pleasure because, if you do it right, you will create a mass of clay that looks like the inside of a conch shell or even an ammonite. At first it may seem bewildering – just how do you create those spirals that emanate from the heart of the clay? (Watching an expert in action may be the best way to pick up this technique – you'll see that every movement is made with intention.) I begin by placing my hands on opposite sides of a roughly rounded lump of clay. Then I use my right hand to push down while rolling it forward. By containing the clay with my left hand, I prevent it from moving sideways. Keeping my feet grounded and my elbows tucked in, I use my core to keep up the rhythm. In a funny way, it reminds me of the cobra pose in yoga with all its amazing benefits: the opening of the heart, stress relief and toning my bum!

As with every other stage of the pottery process, I have to remind myself not to rush and to enjoy the moment. Laziness can sometimes get the better of me and I start to speed up or even try to skip the kneading part. I throw the lump of clay from hand to hand and think, *what damage can the odd air bubble do?* If I'm in this kind of mood, I know I am more likely to hurtle into making the pot at breakneck speed, speed-drying the clay in the sun before shoving it in the kiln. Nine times out of ten this pot won't make it. Maybe it'll be lopsided from throwing clay with lumps in it. Perhaps it'll warp because it has dried too quickly or quite possibly it will just blow up in the kiln – bang! Some lucky pots can survive with air bubbles and only explode because the pot hasn't dried properly. But why take the risk?

Pottery is about balance. It's only now, a good few years into my journey with clay, that I've truly understood what artist and sculptor Barbara Hepworth was talking about in her quote at the start of this chapter. To get the best out of everything I do – whether that's pottery, parenting or painting the shed – I have to be fully engaged with mind, heart, body and soul. Bernard Leach said something similar: 'A potter is one of the few people left who uses his natural faculties of heart, head and hand in balance – the whole man.'[12] These are words from another time and place – but I love the sentiment.

There have been lots of times I've been out of kilter and off-balance – and that's when my body has rebelled and I have become unwell. I'm not saying that's what happened when I had PND, because that hit me out of the blue. With hindsight I can trace a pattern of my body reacting to stress or trauma all the way back to childhood. I was the youngest of four children and frequently had tantrums – the family nicknamed me 'the foghorn'. Those meltdowns left me feeling drained, fatigued and anxious.

Shingles crept over my body when I was six or seven (most cases are in people over 50 years old). Although we'll never know why I got shingles so early, it can be caused by emotional stress. Then, when I was in my early teens, I developed Bell's palsy – a disorder (literally, because your face goes haywire, one side of it falling into a paralysed droop) that baffles professionals. It's possibly caused by inflammation in the body, which makes people with diabetes or autoimmune issues more susceptible to it. Sometimes people catch it after the flu or a viral infection. For the writer Sarah Ruhl, it began in the days after she gave birth to her twins and has lasted for well over a decade, something she writes about in *Smile: The Story of a Face*. Her account of sleep deprivation and how breastfeeding two babies felt like a form of psychosis is painful enough, but all of this she suffered in her words 'with a face she didn't recognise as her own anymore'. She felt that she couldn't smile on the inside, let alone on the outside, at a time when a growing family and the world expects you to smile.

More recently, I was diagnosed with Hashimoto's thyroiditis, another autoimmune disease. In fact, it was just one week after receiving the PND diagnosis – no wonder I felt like shit!

Hashimoto's thyroiditis can lead to serious illness. As well as causing weight gain or loss and exhaustion, it can reduce libido and create difficulties with conception. If it's left untreated it can trigger heart issues or affect your breathing and swallowing as your thyroid gland may swell to form a goitre (a lump in the front of the neck). When I was first diagnosed, I took the prescribed medication, thyroxine. However, when I decided to stop Prozac, I was keen to gently come off thyroxine too and see what happened. I'd had enough of pills.

'It's amazing,' said the doctor when I went back for my blood test results a couple of months later. 'Your thyroid levels are fine.' He went on to say how rare this was and told me to keep doing what I was doing. Admittedly, I had been proactive in my battle against the disease and a big part of staying well had been down to improving my diet and taking regular exercise. I think clay was the key. I'll probably never stop worrying about my thyroid completely. These days, when I am feeling low, agitated or anxious, I know how to channel my emotional energy into clay rather than leave it coursing through my system. I make the comparison between yoga and pottery often as I feel they have the same benefits; one of them being their ability to calm the inner quakes and shakes. The comedian and actor Seth Rogen, a fellow clay enthusiast, feels the same way about pottery: 'It's like yoga, if you got a thing at the end.'[13]

We have no control over what life will throw at us or how our body will respond. Sometimes we only discover our vulnerabilities – which might be mental or physical – when we're challenged. But pottery has brought me a greater understanding of myself. It has facilitated a 'go slow' pedal within. Throwing pots on the wheel has taught me how to centre myself, to listen to my head and my body and be aware when things are in danger of going out of sync.

⚘

After wedging your clay, it is time to throw. At first throwing can seem counterintuitive, a bit like that childhood game of patting your head while rubbing your tummy clockwise. It can just feel very stop-start and disappointing. I initially found it so hard to find my rhythm and every pot I made seemed to end up lopsided or halfway across the room. But Chris Bramble armed me with confidence and encouraged me to persevere. So I did.

Once the clay has been kneaded, it can be placed onto the bat (see Glossary) or slapped directly onto the centre of the wheel. Indulge in that satisfying 'thud' as it hits the wheel's surface. The rounded base of the clay wedge means that no air is trapped when it lands on the wheel. With a bit of practice, you should be able to firmly attach it to the centre of the wheel. Make sure the wheel's surface is not so wet that it slips off – it has to be dry enough that it sticks. I'm right-handed, so I push the elbow of my left arm into my waist and rest my forearm on the tray of the wheel. If you're left-handed, just switch these instructions to the opposite side. You want to be able to easily lean your upper body weight into the clay using your core strength. This is good practice as this gets harder as you become more accomplished and work with bigger pieces of clay.

Using the base of your left hand, push against the lump of clay, add water from a sponge with your right hand and start spinning the wheel with your right foot. The palm of your hand applies the pressure but your fingers are there to squeeze and guide the clay. The edge of your little finger should create a seal between it and the bat, but be careful that it doesn't drag along the base of the wheel. I've done this once or twice and been left with friction burns on the ridge of my finger. The right hand is also creating equal pressure from above, and if the point of contact of your hand on the clay is directly above and the wheel is spinning fast, you should now be centred. If you can still feel a pulse or heartbeat through the clay, then you are not centred. To adjust this, squeeze with the fingers of your left hand and keep pushing your palm firmly against the clay.

Now squeeze your hands together so that the piece of clay turns into a cone-like shape, all the while removing any potential air bubbles that might be left in it. Push the clay back down at a gentle angle, and you should be left with a bread bun shape. Now it's time to turn that bun into the shape of a doughnut by opening up the lump of clay in the centre with your thumbs. Your left hand should always be supporting the lump as both thumbs dig into the clay. Make sure your clay has lots of water running over it so it doesn't stick. Remove your thumbs before they reach the base of the wheel. Spend a moment compressing the base, perhaps with a sponge or rubber kidney (see my toolbox in Chapter 1). Each motion of compressing the clay gives your pot a better chance of surviving the heat of the kiln. You are now centred and it's time pull the walls of the clay upwards to create a cylinder. This cylindrical shape is the springboard for every pot, vase, urn, mug, cup or carafe that begins its life on the wheel.

I'm sure there are all sorts of crafts that can bring together heart, head and hands, keeping everything in balance, but I believe pottery must be one of the most effective. Ultimately, it comes down to touch.

I have talked in earlier chapters about clay having a 'memory', in the sense that it holds the imprint of our emotions and feelings – and I've also touched on the benefits we get from manual activity, and how working with our hands can literally rewire our brains. Here, I am more interested in how touch catalyses the whole-body connection that Bernard Leach speaks of. It is the simple comforting act of touch which, by making a visceral connection between our hands and our head, lights up the pathway to loving, healing and creating. Without touch where would we be?

Handling soft, wet clay brings an almost primaeval joy, one which connects you to the earth and to all the generations before you that have moulded something useful and beautiful from mud deposits near their homes. There is a magical connection to be found from touching fired pottery too – and even rocks and stones. How often have you taken a stone and rubbed its smooth

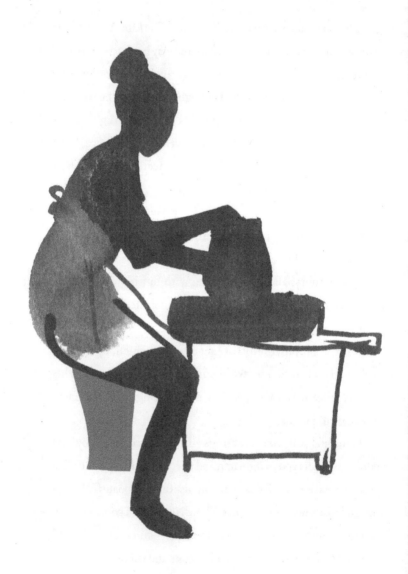

surface before you've thrown it in a river or the sea?

One sunny day in 2021, Henry and I took the children to Henry Moore's Studios and Garden in Hertfordshire to see an exhibition of his work, curated by Edmund de Waal, called 'This Living Hand'. The kids were excited because they were going to be allowed to touch the art. This is a rare privilege and was perhaps something that Moore had in mind when he and his family established the Henry Moore Foundation back in the 1970s. Moore believed that the tactile experience of sculpture was as important as the aesthetic one. So, the iconic bronze sculptures that were on display in the gardens could be touched – albeit with respect. We explained to the children that these hulking pieces of metal might look strong, but they were actually quite fragile as the bronze outer layer was only one centimetre thick. Their eyes lit up as they gently ran their hands over a few of the beautiful forms, before bobbing off to peep through the holes of some of the other epic sculptures.

Sometimes, when I wander around a gallery, I am moved by something totally unexpected. That day, it was a photograph of Moore surrounded by flint. He was obsessed with the shape of flint and many of his sculptures resemble flint stones. Flint had been significant in my life all that summer. We'd spent several weeks at my mother-in-law Henrietta's cottage in Suffolk, and on our country walks and foraging expeditions, we'd found plenty of pointy pieces buried in the earth or jutting out of muddy banks. Flint flushwork covers the walls of my mother-in-law's cottage and all the beautiful old churches in the area. The kids loved looking out for flint pieces in the ground and we all collected some good bits to 'make fires' with. Rubbing the stones together and making sparks fly was brilliant fun for all of us. I have experimented using flint in some of my glaze mixes, so when I saw Moore's affiliation with flint it validated my own growing fascination with mud, rocks and geology.

It was easy to become transfixed by Moore's studies of hands too – the lines, the bend of a finger, the nooks and crannies of the palm as it lies in repose – each one seemed to have its own story to tell. Author Elena Barnabé says 'our hands are the antennas of our soul' and I can certainly see the changes in my own since I became a potter. My fingers are stronger, my palms are getting wider and they are also becoming quite rough. I try not to let it bother me as I'm proud that my hands signify strength and commitment to my art. I always loved my mum's big dependable hands; we call them her spades. All those years of painting, cooking and working in the garden took their toll. I see the beauty in them – a little like Bill Withers in his song 'Grandma's Hands', where the same hands that 'used to ache sometimes and swell,' were also the ones that 'picked me up each time I fell.'

Occasionally, I notice people looking at the veins on the backs of my hands and the cracks in my nails. I'll buy the lotions and potions to look after my face but the rest of my body is only going in one direction, and I'm learning to be okay with that.

The pain I get in my wrist, however, does worry me. Almost all potters will experience wrist, neck and back pain at some stage. Over the years, I've experienced pain at different times, but in the summer of 2021 it became quite bad. I noticed it when I was kneading bread. I remembered during a recent game of tennis I had felt a kind of pop in my hand but ignored it. I played on, but within weeks the pain had stopped play completely. A visit to the doctor's confirmed a case of tennis elbow caused

by overuse of my hand. The doctor was blunt: I had to choose between tennis and pottery. The decision was easy – the tennis 'career' had to be put on hold. So I got a wrist support and hoped it'd get better.

The pain didn't go away, meaning I had to take a break from pottery too. I'm not sure which was worse; my hurting hand or missing the studio. The reality of not being around clay didn't hit me until I went on a trip to Portugal. I had the amazing opportunity to design a line of factory produced ceramics and I went to visit the artisans at work. Just being in that factory and seeing the whole production of my conch shell designs in process was blissful. We watched in wonder as the potters masterfully weaved ribbons of clay to produce lattice pots. As we wandered down the aisles of shelves and surveyed pottery in various stages of production, I felt overwhelmed as I breathed in familiar smells: whiffs of earthy drying clay and the bursts of minerals that make up a glaze. All the time, something inside me was settling and falling back into place. And then, when they let me have a go on the wheel, I had this immense feeling of coming home. When I whipped off the wrist support and got my hands on the clay, I felt the same sense of relief as I did returning home from school as a child. I was home. To feel the mud moving under my hands and my fingers dipping into the cool slip reminded me what I'd been missing.

It wasn't until a few months later, when I started returning to my own studio on a daily basis, that I realised my wrist was beginning to improve. Motion is lotion. Although my body didn't require total rest, it needed to avoid any aggressive actions involved in repetitive throwing. My hands were yearning for the gentle motion of kneading and creating to bring back some strength. Since then, I've learned to listen to my body: that sublime feeling that overcame me in the factory in Portugal was the one to chase.

✡

I was recently struck by the story of a pottery studio in the USA in which clay is used to express the pain and frustration of living with cancer. One potter created her own little clay army of breast cancer survivors – it was one of the ways she dealt with her own mastectomy and reconstruction surgery. In a similar way, when contestant Christine Cherry presented her abstract self-portrait in the final of the *Great Pottery Throw Down* in 2022, it was hard not to shed tears with judge Keith Brymer Jones. Christine is a breast cancer survivor and her simple sculpture, with its hole where her breast once was, was brave, beautiful, dignified and defiant. Christine's words engraved along the back took my breath away: 'Never be ashamed of a scar. It shows a battle won'.

In ancient Greece, women used to make large vases called

pithoi. These earthenware vessels were used for holding anything from wine to wheat. Sometimes they were even used as coffins, which gives you an idea of how enormous they could be. Freya (Chris's daughter and my pottery partner in crime) and I have made some pretty hefty pots together, but we have never attempted anything as big as that. Apparently, they were often made on the wheel. The mind boggles at how they did this, but there was probably a gang of potters working together. In 2009, the skeleton of a woman dating from the first millennium BC was discovered on the Greek island of Crete, and when scientists studied her remains, they found some very unusual signs of wear and tear. Here was a person who was completely misaligned; with over developed muscles on her right side and the cartilage on her hips and knees worn away.

It took some time to work out what had caused these anomalies. It was only when they studied the bones of other artisans, such as weavers and potters, that it became clear. Those muscles on the right had developed from constantly leaning on one side as the clay was spinning on the wheel – imagine the strength she needed to manoeuvre those big pots. The cartilage around her poor bones was probably worn away as she kicked the wheel into action over and over again.

I can't help thinking of that woman and what she went through all those thousands of years ago. If there's anything I'd recommend, it's to listen to your own body as much a possible. By listening, you will be naturally checking in with your head and your heart.

FLEA BITES

- How does touching the clay make you feel? Perhaps the cool, somewhat clammy texture feels strange at first. Notice how the clay warms up as you knead and play with it. Try adding more water – does the gluey slip mean your piece falls apart, or does it take on a life of its own? Go on a journey with your clay and acknowledge its changes along the way so you begin to understand its properties.

- As you mould the clay, try to discover which shapes you are drawn to or repeat so you begin to know yourself a little better too. I often fall into the same patterns – some of which can be harmful – but when I recognise them I can change, grow and be healthier in body and spirit.

- Breathing exercises are calming and help to still a racing heart or mind. In yoga we're encouraged to breathe and use visualisation to open up the space within our bodies. The clay and sandplay therapist Lynne Souter-Anderson suggests doing breath work while kneading clay. It's best to do this with your eyes closed so you can concentrate on the feel of the clay as you count your breaths in and out. Start simply and count to six as you breathe in, pause, then count to six as you breathe out. I find it makes me calmer and more in touch with the clay and just a little less conscious of what's affecting me in the outside world. Once you arrive in this safe space, allow your fingers to do what they want. Who knows what they will do when your mind is concentrating on counting the breaths rather than worrying about other things?

- When it comes to throwing on the wheel, it's important to learn the basic rules, but equally to follow your instinct and use your intuition. Make every movement with intention. The moment I lose confidence, the vase goes flying across the room.

- For a passionate description of the transformative and spiritual feelings evoked by throwing on the wheel, listen to Edmund de Waal on BBC's *Desert Island Discs* podcast. In a toss-up between writing and pottery, he admits to always choosing pottery.

- Learning to throw is much like learning to play a musical

instrument; there are certain chords that are crucial in creating your masterpiece. After you've learned those chords, it's time to be playful. Try throwing blindfolded, or with one hand; spin the wheel in the wrong direction or throw using your toes.

- Gregory Tingay is a master potter and former pupil of Bernard Leach, who teaches at Studio Pottery London. If you book a session with him he will encourage you to try out multiple positions in order to find your comfort zone when throwing. 'Arms can be placed on your knees or on the basin of the wheel when centring. Firm anchorage is crucial to this process', he says.

5

BUILDING STRONG WALLS

'Out of the fire comes firmness, through stress we pass to strength.'

CHARLES F. BINNS, CERAMICIST

I love working with the clay from Grand Bahama Island, where I lived, worked and learned to forage for clay in the wild. It has a beautiful rich-red colour that makes me wonder what it will look like when it's fired. It feels cool as I drop it onto the centre of the wheel. At first, my hands do very little as the wheel whirls round and I position my body to centre the clay. Moments later, the void in front of me is filling with the spinning clay that slowly begins to form into a vessel. It's mesmerising and I can lose myself in these moments.

I have this vision in my head – an elegant, long-necked vase with a wide, open rim like the leaves of a water lily. This vessel needs to be robust enough to hold water, so it needs strong, even walls.

Instinctively, when I know the moment is right, I squeeze the water from the wet sponge onto the spinning lump of clay and slowly dig my thumbs deep into the surface. The clay yields to my fingers and I'm away. My hands glide over the silky sides of the vessel as it forms. Next, I move my right hand to the base and wrap it firmly around its circumference. As my other hand sweeps upwards, I form a stable, rigid cylinder – I think it will survive the blasting heat of the kiln. First it needs to be bone dry.

I've been contemplating my pot as it stands awaiting its turn in the kiln. Its colour has faded to a burnt umber and it feels as fragile as a child's hand. This vessel has been on quite a journey already – from a lump of foraged clay to a fine sculpture. Now it's about to enter the inferno. It's vulnerable and I feel protective. But the next stage is essential if we are to realise the full and lasting beauty of the pot – as ever, part of a mother's love is letting go… 'I did my best, I built strong walls.' I place it in the kiln and hope with all my heart.

———

I am always hit by a sense of wonder when a truly beautiful pot comes out of the kiln. I inspect its curves, gaze at the glaze and marvel at how it's worked out – and sometimes how it hasn't – but is still a lovely object. Anything and everything can go wrong in the process, but when you get it right, it's wonderful. Lucie Rie sees it as a voyage of discovery: 'To make pottery is an adventure to me, every new work is a new beginning.'

Once the pots are bone dry, they are placed in the kiln for a biscuit firing at 1000 degrees C. At this point they are removed from the kiln, but they are still very delicate and the surface feels porous, like pumice stone. They can be gently fettled and then glazed, before they are returned back into the fiery depths of the kiln for their final blast, for which the temperature gauge is raised to a terrific 1260 degrees C. After an intense ten hours, you turn the kiln off and leave it to come back to room temperature – this can take up to twelve hours. I usually get butterflies as I wait for the kiln to cool down. Then, when I lift the lid, it's like 'the big reveal'. What has happened to my creations, especially my delicate sculptures, during the firing process? Sometimes, my pieces are paper thin yet somehow they survive the heat of the kiln, and the subsequent cool-down. A third firing is sometimes necessary for gold lustre or enamelling at 700–750 degrees C.

I love to push the clay to the limit and see where it takes me, but it is always a thrill to create something that has strength as well as fragility. That vase I made with the water lily neck has become one of my personal favourites – simple, solid and in my eyes perfect. I've since made three of them and gifted them to friends and family. There is a magic about pottery. Whatever alchemy is involved, I think the secret is building strong walls – whether you throw your pot on the wheel, or make it with coils by hand – those walls are the key to its resilience.

So how do you go about creating these wonder walls? It all starts at the beginning when you're kneading or wedging the clay, because good compression at this stage makes the clay stronger and less likely to crack or warp when it's drying or goes in the kiln. It's vital, too, to build walls of equal thickness – you don't want a fat base and thin walls, because although it seems counterintuitive, a heavy base doesn't actually support the walls of the pot any better. In time, your hands will know instinctively when the walls are uniform, so practice does make perfect. But if you're ever in doubt, pull your pot a little more or pinch and refine its shape until it's as thin as possible. Of course, you can go too far and sabotage the vessel but again this is a good way to learn. Another tip is to use your rubber kidney tool to smooth and compress the clay as you go. As well as intuitively getting to know your pot with your fingers, you'll get an eye for what's right, so always look inside the pot to check the walls. Some pottery teachers will insist upon slicing your pre-fired pots in half to demonstrate how well you've evened up the walls. I can almost hear the shouts of 'What, really?' It's a sacrificial act for sure, but one you'll never forget. It's a good lesson, too, in the art of letting some of your hard work go – some pots should have L-plates pinned to them – they were never meant to be keepers.

✿

When PND hit me after the birth of Iris, I had to make a very conscious decision to rebuild my own walls – I don't mean walls to avoid feeling pain; I mean strong walls to use as foundations and as pillars that would protect me from whatever life threw at me. I discovered a whole new set of tools for survival in the long term. Counselling, exercise and of course venturing to my first pottery classes were part of the kit. I also learned to become more self-accepting and to treat myself with more compassion. Looking back, I realise that these building blocks helped me through the next chapter of motherhood too, and the very real challenges it brought.

Our little boy Jimmy was born in late November. After the post natal trauma we both endured following my first pregnancy, Henry and I decided that we wanted to be prepared in every way possible – which meant knowing if our baby was a girl or a boy. Pregnancy was just as exciting the second time around; I used one of those baby-tracking apps so I could picture the baby growing inside me – one week he was the size of a sunflower seed, and before I knew it, I was carrying a watermelon. I still had my modelling hat on when I was pregnant with Iris, so I wore pretty dresses and worried about gaining too much weight – if you'd been walking behind me, you'd never have guessed that there was a 'baby on board'. With Jimmy, I would joke that my face seemed to be swallowing up my eyes. The stretch marks arrived too, but I learned not to mind. My mindset had changed and I was all the stronger for it. But, and this is a massive BUT, I was petrified I'd get PND again. No matter how strong I thought I was, a demon was sitting on my shoulder asking me 'What if you get ill again?'

I wonder how many women who only have one baby would cite PND as the reason for not having more? There are so many questions around the subject – maybe it's time we started a wider conversation and brought it out into the open. Although some celebrities have spoken openly about their struggles with PND, many women continue to suffer in silence, perhaps due to the continuing stigma around mental health issues. Louis Theroux's 2019 documentary *Mothers on the Edge* was a hard watch for me, but it was enlightening hearing mothers talking so honestly about their postpartum mental health. I imagine many viewers were surprised by some of the cases filmed at specialist wards; new mothers talking about suicide or discussing their lack of bonding with their baby is an uncomfortable reality.

Theroux tried hard to understand what was happening to

these women; at times even I found it difficult to comprehend and I've been there. But this harrowing documentary reminded me how real and tragic this illness can be. It can stop you living life to the full and sometimes that includes having the family you may have dreamed about.

Before trying for another baby, Henry and I had researched the odds of getting PND again. In fact, research suggests that if you had PND with your first baby, you're more likely to have it again, but risks vary dramatically from about 30 to 70 per cent.[14] Numbers like that are scary and I wanted more reassurance. This is where women can help one another. By telling our stories about childbirth and being honest about our experiences others will have more information to hand. We can learn from each others' situations and make more informed choices for future pregnancies. I found that reading about how other people coped definitely helped me to build strong walls and inspired me to keep going. These women were willing to take the gamble, and so was I.

I had discovered I was pregnant with Jimmy in an unglamorous, run-down Bahamian casino. My best friend Cosima was there to share the excitement, but it wasn't long before I was internalising my next dilemma – should I stop taking Prozac now I was pregnant?

Of course, it was straight back on the internet, scrolling for information about antidepressants and their effects on unborn babies. Scientific reports and medical papers don't make good reading. If you look hard enough, you'll find the ones that link taking antidepressants with a higher risk of birth problems – so I almost threw the pills down the loo right then.

As I carried on researching, I found other reports stating that the evidence was just observational. My decision to continue taking Prozac was not taken lightly. I talked it through with my doctor and with friends who had taken antidepressants. I thought long and hard about what I was going to do. And, of course, I discussed it with Henry and my family. One of the most important messages I gathered from reading about other women's experiences was the need to look after my own mental health, so I would be capable of looking after our child. If I unravelled, it would have an effect on our entire family – the walls could come crashing down.

An epidural-free birth was now also off the cards. After twice-botched epidurals with Iris, I was determined to be in the right headspace with my second child. Our birth plan looked very different this time, and we opted in advance for an epidural if it was needed. To my surprise, I found the early stages of labour much more manageable second time round, almost enjoyable – I was the semi-natural earth mother I had always wanted to be. I felt so confident and in control that I nearly convinced myself that I didn't need the epidural after all. It was my sister Christabel who reminded me that there is a point of no return 'Just have the epidural before it's too late,' she urged me, 'before the pain is too intense.'

So we went for it, and Jimmy was born, this big, beautiful healthy boy. The joy of our new baby was just as immense the second time, but, because the birth had been managed so well, I felt more present. There was time and there was a real sense of calm, as Henry and I both savoured the delicious smell of our newborn. The memory is so clear, that warm and cosy feeling as I held him close to my chest – a moment that will be treasured for ever.

Some hours after the birth, the consultant came through and explained that Jimmy had a little 'crackle' on his chest, possibly caused by inhaling amniotic fluid when he came out. He said it wasn't serious or anything to worry about. Perhaps the Prozac helped protect me against panicking at that moment. Our families visited and Iris sang to her little brother. It was November and there was a chill in the air, but my new baby and I were safe and comfortable, cocooned in that room, and Henry and I were looking forward to bringing him home.

The first couple of weeks were blissful and Jimmy was clearly a contented baby. We were just beginning to go out for strolls with him in his buggy. The weather was cold, but we dressed warmly and he was swaddled in blankets. Everything seemed okay. But then, just after he'd turned two weeks old, Jimmy caught a cold. To begin with it was just sniffles and nobody was particularly worried. The memory of laying him down to sleep in his cot is still etched in my mind. He looked so peaceful – I had no inkling of what was about to happen.

'You need to call the hospital.' Only half an hour after I'd laid Jimmy down in his cot, the silhouette of Maura, our nanny, appeared at our bedroom door. I couldn't see her face but I could tell by her voice that she was worried. 'Jimmy isn't right,' she said. 'His breathing is all wrong and he's making these strange noises.'

I ran to the landing and she gently placed him in my arms. It was clear he was not okay; his rosy pink cheeks had turned a muted dull colour and he was making this terrible wheezing sound. Every time he tried to gasp for air, I felt more anxious. I began to wail. Henry was on the phone immediately.

The ambulance arrived within three minutes. Paramedics stormed through the house to rescue our child. Everything that followed is a blur. The paramedics gently placed Jimmy on the sofa and his tiny babygrow, the one I had put on after his bath a few hours earlier, was sliced down the middle with a pair of scissors. His little body looked grey and you could see his lungs beneath his ribcage struggling to take in oxygen.

The paramedics were too focused on Jimmy to answer

our questions, but the gravity of the situation was written on everybody's face. Jimmy's little body was loaded onto an adult stretcher and we were rushed to St. Mary's Hospital. Inside the ambulance, he was wired up to all kinds of apparatus and he had an enormous mask on his little face. I recall the stark lights on the inside of the ambulance and the whirl of flashing blue on the outside. It felt so lonely, like I was watching all this happen to us from above.

'Please, please let him be okay,' I repeated in my head as the paramedics pulled up at the hospital. Outside, the freezing December air was biting and Jimmy was naked and lying on the stretcher without anything covering him. Surely that would make him worse? My teeth were chattering and I was shivering as the cold and fear set in.

Henry was there beside me as we were rushed into the emergency room and ushered to one side as doctors and nurses crowded around our baby. Everything switched up a gear as the whole team sprang into action. There were shouts of, 'Get the ketamine'. Isn't that a party drug? I was shocked because I didn't know they gave these drugs to seriously ill babies. Everything happened quickly, but I remember hearing someone say, 'We can't get a line in.' I found little comfort in the faces of the consultants.

Next, they used what looked like a large drill to get a line into Jimmy's tiny shin.

He had been placed in an induced coma. This was the only way forward. The doctors had to increase his oxygen intake to keep him alive. He was taken upstairs to the Paediatric Intensive Care Unit (PICU), the beating heart of the hospital, where they would attempt to save his life.

That night was hell. Henry left in the early hours to be with Iris. Somehow, I snatched a bit of sleep on the sofa in the common room but I woke up bleary, with my cheek stuck to the plastic chair. Reality kicked me in the face again – my newborn son was desperately ill, in a coma, wired up to all kinds of life-saving equipment, yet I was powerless to help him or hold him close – my child's life was in the hands of the doctors and I had to trust and believe that they would make him better. 'Stay calm, Flea,' I told myself and I fell back on my deep-breathing exercises to keep a grip on the swirling emotions inside.

I think that Prozac played a big part in keeping me semi-anchored – so much so that I was slightly adrift from the reality of the situation, which possibly helped me at the time. Simultaneously, I was also tapping into an inner strength that comes with being a mother. I once heard a story about a woman who moved a car to save her child – who knows if it really happened – but I understood that sentiment: I would have done anything to protect my child.

The doctors diagnosed Jimmy with bronchiolitis. It is a

common infection of the lungs and airways in children under two years old. It's usually caused by the respiratory syncytial virus (RSV), which is rampant during the damp British wintertime. In most cases, it is a mild illness that can be treated at home but now there is some evidence that SARS-CoV-2 might cause a more severe form of bronchiolitis requiring hospitalisation. At the time of Jimmy's illness, he was one of the 3 per cent who needed hospital care. Statistics are not easy reading; each year around 33 million people infected with RSV worldwide will have serious chest infections. It will cause about 60,000 deaths in children under five, with half of those deaths in children under six months old.[15] I might not have stayed so calm if I had known the statistics then.

Somehow, I was focused on Jimmy and his battle for survival. It turned out that the 'crackle' Jimmy had at birth had made him more susceptible to chest infections. Coughs and sneezes that circulate every winter, which are pretty harmless to most of us, could be fatal to him. The fact that he had caught the virus even when we were cosily tucked up at home was frightening. Fortunately for us, we had arrived at the hospital just in time for Jimmy to receive the treatment he desperately needed to survive.

The next few days were a blur. Jimmy remained stable but he was still on life support. Henry and I took turns at his bedside. That tiny common room, with its leatherette sofa and endless supply of tea and biscuits, became our sanctuary. I do remember a visit from Henry's cousin, who is a paediatric doctor at the Cromwell Hospital. Like everybody in the family, he wanted to help us if he could. He reassured us that we were in the best hands. We had faith in the NHS and the wonderful medical staff at St. Mary's, but it felt good to have a second opinion. He also suggested that we shouldn't stay in the common room too long and to keep the windows open, to reduce the risk of Jimmy catching another virus. Post-pandemic, it's amazing to think how much more aware we are of the way viruses spread; particularly in confined spaces with lots of people passing through. Now we wouldn't think twice about throwing open the windows and doors, and we accept the stricter rules around hospital visits.

After six days, things suddenly looked better. The specialists said they were thinking of bringing Jimmy out of his induced coma. It felt like a miracle and, for the first time since Jimmy's admission, I was able to go home for longer than an hour. I could cuddle Iris and could take her for a hot chocolate in the park. But a late-night call from a nurse telling us to get to the hospital immediately shattered this false sense of security. I immediately gathered myself together and went back to the hospital on my own, while Henry stayed with Iris.

I've never felt so alone as in that moment when I first saw Jimmy again. As soon as I arrived at St. Mary's, the staff rushed me up to the PICU, where a team of doctors and nurses were working on him as he lay in the bed. Jimmy's lungs had collapsed. He was having a pulmonary haemorrhage and was bleeding into his lungs. My little boy was lying there, helpless, under a pool of lights. Strangely, Caravaggio's painting *Sleeping Cupid* came to mind. Beautiful, untouchable but real – so small, weak and distant.

I realise now that the call from the nurses that night was so I could say goodbye to him. I'm not sure when the gravity of it all hit me, but without doubt this was easily the worst thing that had ever happened in my life. That night, in those dark moments at the hospital, I was held by strangers – the hospital staff and the parents of other children who, like angels, supported me.

Slowly, Jimmy pulled through. Every step of his recovery was harrowing; watching him come off the drugs he'd been given to stay alive was horrible. After another five days, the doctors felt he was strong enough to come off the morphine, and he was moved to the rehab ward. By now, I could hold Jimmy again, but it was torturous to watch him in pain. The atmosphere in the new ward was different. The doctors here only did the rounds a few times a day and suddenly we felt quite alone. At least we had visits from both our families. One of my loveliest memories is of Iris and Maura, our guardian angel, singing sweet lullabies to Jimmy.

Jimmy came home just before Christmas. It felt so good to

have my little family all together under the same roof. The relief was immense but so was the worry – it's something that
will never leave me totally. Nor will the questions. I try not
to, but as humans we are guilty of speculating… what would
have happened to Jimmy had we not checked on him at that
moment in the middle of the night? I feel lucky every day that
things happened the way they did, and that we had the NHS to
rely on.

⚜

I still can't drive past St. Mary's Hospital without thinking
about how Jimmy's life was saved there. Neither can I forget
the other children who were fighting terrible illnesses on the
PICU. I often think of the children and parents who are there
right now – strangers to me but I understand the pain they are
experiencing, and I hope they are finding the strength they need
to get through it. During Jimmy's hospital stay, we found plenty
of comfort in strangers. There were just ten beds on the PICU
and each was occupied by a severely ill child. In a matter of days,
we became close to many of their parents. We were there for
each other when the doctors did the rounds and new develop-
ments had to be processed. We all experienced some shattering
emotional moments, and there was this feeling that we were in
it together. We couldn't help but be affected by the bravery we
witnessed: of the doctors who fought for our children's lives (and

had to make horrendously difficult decisions in the process), of the little children in pain and of the parents who had to grieve for their old lives and accept a new reality.

I also wonder how I coped. I know that Prozac played its part but so did the inner strength that I'd been working towards since my first bout of depression. Whenever I take a pot out of the kiln, I'm reminded that, with strong walls, those 'pillars of strength', I can survive life's infernos. I've discovered that the depths of hell are manageable and that survival feels empowering.

Louise Bourgeois, one of my favourite artists, conveyed the pain of her troubled childhood through sculptures and installations. She also captured how I feel about this time in my life in her famous quote: 'I've been to hell and back and let me tell you it was wonderful.' Nothing about Jimmy's illness was 'wonderful', but surviving that hell gave me a different perspective and I have seen the world through new eyes ever since.

FLEA BITES

- People – like pots – need to be strong to survive life. I often felt weak and powerless and didn't know how to begin the insurmountable task of becoming more resilient. I love the Chinese saying: 'a journey of a thousand miles begins with a single step'. You can only build your wall brick by brick, and this takes time and practice.

- Depression is lonely but you don't have to be isolated. It took strength to admit I had a problem and just a little more courage to reach out and ask for help. Real strength isn't pretending you're okay; it's admitting you're not.

- Tools are helpful in building strong walls. Routine, exercise, deep breathing and finding an occasional quiet space just for you are part of the kit. My mantra is 'wheel time = time for me'. Hopefully you'll find something you love doing that makes your confidence grow.

- The key to making strong walls in pottery is ensuring the sides are the same width from the top to the bottom of your vessel. This applies whether you are working on or off the wheel. Learning how to do this is a bit like mastering a musical instrument – it takes time and regular practice. To build strong walls on the wheel you need to reinforce the clay with your index fingers and a sponge as you pull up. Watch how much water you use. Too much and the clay will flop. Too little and it will be too dry, causing your fingers to skid and the pot to collapse. It's a fine balance, but when you build that strong-walled vessel, the feeling of satisfaction will be immense.

6

TOTALLY THROWN

'Siblings are like potters; they try you by fire, glaze you with taunts, finish you with well-aimed jibes. If you emerge from the kiln without cracking, you can survive the world.'

LISA TAKEUCHI CULLEN, *PASTOR'S WIVES*

Why the hell did I agree to be on a reality TV show?

My heart is pounding and I'm trying hard to breathe steadily. I'm in the green room with eleven lovely potters from across the UK. We're a mixed bag of age, gender and background, but we're united by a love of clay. We all look a bit pale and shaky because we're waiting to be called in for the first challenge on *The Great Pottery Throw Down*.

Each episode has two challenges: the 'Main Make', which potters can prepare for during the week before filming, and the undercover 'Throw Down' challenge, which launches you straight in the deep end as you have no idea what's coming. In the other room, we can hear the production team getting everything ready for the mystery 'Throw Down' challenge.

Who knows what they have in store for us?

I strain my ears to hear the camera crew setting set up. Am I ready to do this? I've been rehearsing for weeks, studying endless previous episodes and taking directions from my pal Freya who's already been on the show. I've worked on the wheel, practised my hand building and researched glaze recipes, but nothing could prepare me for these jitters.

'ACTION,' the producer calls, and finally we're led through to the studio. Everything feels a bit hazy, but presenter Melanie Sykes makes her entrance and I try to focus on the rows of workbenches. I can see the twelve wheels, but it's the dust sheets and what's underneath them that's puzzling me. I make my way to my table where my very own lump of 'something' is waiting. Everyone goes quiet as the judges walk in, and I swallow the nerves. Pottery judge Sue Pryke looks immaculate and judge Keith Brymer Jones is wearing his denim dungarees with nothing underneath. I can't help but smile… maybe he's channelling Patrick Swayze's topless look in that scene from *Ghost*. It's amazing what will pop into your head when you're feeling tense. At least it helps to calm my nerves a little.

'Right,' says Keith. The atmosphere is charged. 'I want you

to make as many egg cups, thrown off the hump, as you can in fifteen minutes.' What a relief! I'm smiling on the inside because I've been 'throwing off the hump' all week, making knobs for my teapot. I can hear Sue giving her instructions but my head is already getting set. By the time Mel wishes us good luck, I'm off.

All those years of taking a 'vite et mal' approach to my French studies are coming to fruition here. 'Quantity not necessarily quality' is the specification the judges have given us. Eating boiled eggs and soldiers as a child stands me in good stead too, as I am able to picture those little egg cups and this somehow gives me some focus. I feel calmer and ready for action.

Luckily, they have prepared the enormous hump for us and the clay is already centred – result! This is a major relief as I just don't think I could centre 20kg of clay now, especially under the glare of the cameras and the judges. Instead, I can focus on the top half of the clay, which feels soft and silky – the perfect texture for throwing the egg cups. As the wheel spins my hands begin to take over and I forget about how scared I'm feeling. The camera crew and fellow contestants fall away into the distance. The remaining nervous energy is in my favour and the autopilot kicks in. I'm in the zone, doing my thing. WHOOOOOOOOOSH. Wow, it feels good as my fingers dip and smooth the clay to create each little cup.

Suddenly, as if by magic (and I guess a little experience),

the great hump of clay has produced loads of curvy little cups of roughly the same size. I'm working too quickly to count but there's a fair number of them and, at a glance, they seem well formed. I can hear the other potters' wheels humming and the occasional yelp or sigh. There just isn't time to look around and see what they're up to. 'I can feel the tension in the room,' says Keith. This is the only challenge that must be done in one take – there's no going back or opportunity to repeat it – so I stay in my zone. Until the buzzer goes off. Really? That was quick.

'Step away from your wheels,' Keith cuts in, and I stand back to look at what I've produced. I feel happy with my collection of cups lined up on the workbench. There are roughly twenty of them and they look pretty consistent and upright. I scan the room to see what everyone else has done. I daren't hope too much – I mean, you just don't…

Sue and Keith give each potter's egg cups a once-over. Quite a few end up in the reject bucket – there's a squelch as Keith's fist comes down on a misfit cup. One way of testing the functionality is seeing if an egg sits perfectly in the cup. Even though my fellow contestant Kit has been brought up surrounded by hens and their eggs, he's found this challenge tricky and some of his cups look more like goblets for ostrich eggs.

By the time the judges make their way to me, it's obvious there's a clear winner, and I'm genuinely gobsmacked. That's when my tears begin. I'm crying as if I've won the whole competition – like Leona Lewis when she won *The X Factor*, FFS! In my head I'm delighted but I'm harbouring other stuff. A hurricane hit the Bahamas a few days ago. Henry has rushed home to help. It's a disaster for the island – homes, businesses and lives have been lost. I'm grieving because my dog Maggie drowned during the storm. Life on the island is in turmoil. I'm thrilled to win this challenge but my tears are also for the devastation at home.

And then all the potters circle around and hug me. We have only known each other for a day or two, but we feel bonded already. As they envelop me in their arms, pat me with their muddy hands, and congratulate me so sincerely, the WHOOSH returns and everything feels okay again.

———

Throwing off the hump... If you don't know anything about pottery then this has to be one of the strangest expressions – a combination of getting the hump and throwing things around, it sounds something like a teenage tantrum. It's actually the perfect way of making multiples of the same thing, usually something small such as dainty tea cups, tiny bowls, door knobs, maybe even buttons in one session. Also, once you hit your stride, it's

a quick and satisfying way of working. It begins with one great lump or hump of clay, which needs to be centred on your wheel. The good thing about this technique is you only have to centre the giant piece of clay once, at the beginning.

When it is centred, you use your thumb and fingers to raise a small cone of clay, which you then shape and smooth into the vessel you desire. I'd say the trickiest part is gauging how thick you need the bottom of your vessel to be, because it's difficult to judge when your pot is still conjoined to the big lump of clay below. The final step is cutting the pot off from the rest of the clay – and this is the part I find most satisfying. You'll need knives and cutting wires at the ready for this step and you'll have to watch you don't squeeze or squish your pot too tight or misjudge the cut in the process. Everything is spinning and moving quickly, so it's not easy. It takes tons of practice, but eventually it becomes second nature – well, cross my muddy fingers it does.

Again, it's useful to watch other potters at work. Keith Brymer Jones does it effortlessly, and I was lucky enough to watch him in action when I was on the set of *The Great Pottery Throw Down*. Search online and you'll find master and budding potters from all over the globe throwing off the hump and giving it a go. Prepare to be mesmerised and quite possibly inspired to try it yourself. I was intrigued to discover old footage of Simon Leach, the grandson of the famous potter Bernard Leach, doing it a few decades ago. At this stage, he was unsure of the process and said as much when he addressed his viewers and asked them to contact him with tips for getting it right. Flash forward to 2021 and he's making egg cups using small balls of clay he places directly on the wheel, so perhaps throwing off the hump just wasn't for him.

You don't have to throw off the hump to produce a large number of pots in record time. If you want to see a real master in action, there is stunning black-and-white footage on YouTube from the early 1960s of 'country potter' Isaac Button when he was about 70.[16] Modern potters like Chris Bramble and Keith Brymer Jones cite this wily Yorkshireman as an inspiration. Even Bernard Leach once asked for his advice, apparently. Isaac lived just outside Halifax and whisked up a million pots at his own pottery studio on Soil Hill (place names like this usually give a hint of what the area was associated with in the past). No doubt he was a dab hand at throwing off the hump too, but I love watching as his delicate but dexterous hands morph a fist-sized ball of clay into a sturdy little pot within seconds. In fact, it takes him just 22 seconds to throw the clay, make the pot and cut it off the wheel. And then he makes another – in the words of Tommy Cooper, 'just like that'.

It's said that on a typical day Isaac could turn a ton of clay into 1200 household pots – functional ware for cooking, dining,

storing or for potting plants. Most of these were fit for purpose. They had to be – this was his livelihood. Some of Isaac's pots sold for as little as a few pence back then, so it was a numbers game for him. The quest for quantity didn't mean he compromised on quality. At the time, his pots may have been considered almost throwaway, but you'll pay upwards of £30 for one of his small jugs now – many of which have stood the test of time and pop up on eBay. They may not have Lucie Rie's delicate touch, but they're trusty and rustic and evoke another time, prior to plastic, when pottery held its place in the home.

I love going to places in the world where pottery still has the upper hand. In Mumbai, the chai wallahs (tea sellers) used to serve tea in earthenware cups called *kulhads*. One of my most vivid memories from when I visited India was of drinking from one of these little clay cups, then just throwing it down to the ground when I'd finished. Roads were strewn with orange-red broken bits of clay which were eventually ground down by footfall into the earth from which they came. This environmentally friendly way of serving chai has been replaced by glass, and in more recent years by paper or plastic cups. I believe that some places are trying to return to the old way of doing things, recognising that those little clay cups help look after the planet and boost the pottery industry.

In another reel, Isaac Button is creating an enormous vessel for storing ale or cider (much better for our environment than plastic bottles). It's half his size yet he's able to smooth it into shape quickly and efficiently while keeping a steady grip on the pipe in his mouth, which is a skill in itself as sometimes the pipe looks perilously close to falling into the pot. Once he's done, he offers a jolly smile and takes a big puff – you can really sense his satisfaction. He loved an ale too and said of himself that he never left the pub the same day he entered it. He foraged for clay and ran his own coal-fired kiln.

Although it was thrilling to win the 'throwing off the hump' challenge on *The Great Pottery Throw Down*, it's not a technique

I go for regularly these days. I am more cautious of straining my hands and wrists with too much repetitive work. But the idea of all these pots being created from one hunk of clay is very appealing – in the same way that families are made from the same stuff and often share common traits!

If ever one family could be described as 'thrown off the hump', it must be the Leach clan – with many of the family involved with pottery or the arts in some way. Bernard Leach, the so-called father of British studio pottery, lived a long and clay-fulfilled life, passing away in 1979 at the age of 92. Incidentally, lots of potters seem to make it to old age (Lucie Rie 93, Betty Woodman 87 and Michael Cardew 82). Leach is credited with bridging Western and Eastern pottery practice. He founded Leach Pottery in St. Ives, Cornwall, in 1920 with the assistance of the Japanese master potter, Shoji Hamada.[17] He was almost evangelical about creating simple and utilitarian earthenware, and his reputation lives on not just in his pottery but also through his descendants.

His sons David and Michael were first off the hump, with David doing an apprenticeship with his father before training in pottery management at Stoke-on-Trent. He introduced electricity and an oil-fired kiln to Leach Pottery and later started his own Lowerdown Pottery at Bovey Tracey in Devon. Younger son Michael studied natural science before being lured back to

help with the family business in the 1930s. During the Second World War, he served with the army in Uganda, where he set up a commercial pottery practice, making utensils for the troops. Later he set up his own Yelland Pottery at Fremington in Devon.

Pottery runs in the blood of Bernard's grandchildren too. Michael's son Philip tried to evade the family business by escaping to Tehran in Iran to work at an American school. Inevitably, clay got its claws in when he became fascinated with Persian ceramics (those vibrant blues!) and so he started teaching pottery there. He later founded Springfield Pottery in Hartland, Devon,

with his wife Frannie. Meanwhile, David's son Simon Leach –
he of the 'egg cups not thrown off the hump' fame – learned
his art at his father's pottery at Lowerdown. These days he's
throwing his own pottery in the USA – ensuring that the Leach
name, as well as all that pottery know-how, travels near and far.

The Leach family has taken a fairly united path. But, in pottery terms, throwing off the hump does not necessarily mean
striving for uniformity. In Japan, in particular, certain styles
of ceramics made in this way celebrate difference and are more
inclined to take on a life of their own – a little off centre maybe
but beautiful nevertheless. Likewise, if a potter is making a set
of bowls for drinking tea (*chawan*), each vessel is considered
an individual piece with its own personality expressed through
its unique form or glaze. I like this idea and find it helps me in
other areas of my life, like parenting. It also gives me a good
perspective on my own past.

Since becoming a potter, I've spent a lot of time thinking
about how things are formed, and by extension how we become
the people we are. We are partly defined by our environment
and the labels we get lumbered with. When you hear these labels
long enough you start to believe them. They can define you,
and you make decisions based on them. On the other hand,
though, some things just happen or fall into our laps and we go
for them because we're young and inexperienced and, well, some

things just sound so exciting and tempting.

That was how I started modelling. It was the end of the 1990s, long before mobile phones and Instagram. Kate Moss was 'the world's hottest supermodel' and the model agencies were looking for skinny, adolescent girls to follow in her footsteps. I was fourteen when a scout approached me outside Topshop on Oxford Street. Of course, it was thrilling and confidence boosting. But it was an instant 'No way!' from my mum. Eventually, when I was seventeen, I persuaded her to let me see what was involved. With my shape and size, I was like a functional piece of pottery, so the calls for commercial castings came thick and fast. Before long I was getting lots of catalogue jobs. Back then you could make two thousand pounds as a day rate, which was a small fortune and seventeen-year-old me thought I could retire in no time.

Soon I was doing TV adverts, which was when I really hit my stride. I could tap into my inner drama queen without having to learn a long script. Often I'd just have to remember a few lines and barely act at all. Wafting around a room filled with white balloons in an ad for the bookmaker, Paddy Power, was a laugh, and the money I earned from these jobs meant that I could start collecting art and spend happy afternoons in auction houses. But it wasn't long before the doubts crept in. I felt scrutinised and was sometimes criticised by both modelling agents and clients. Looking back, I can see there was nothing wrong with my body, but my teenage self didn't find it so easy to bat the nasty comments away.

Modelling is such an up-and-down career and it's not an ideal job if you are someone who struggles with your mental health. It was at this time that I started to develop an anxiety about being in front of the camera.

It returned with gusto a few years later, when the paparazzi followed me around during a brief relationship with someone in the public eye. I experienced panic attacks and those feelings of anxiety still return from time to time. As my pottery business has grown, I've had to create a website and social media presence. Some days, I find the public-facing side of pottery difficult. Given my feelings about being in front of the camera, accepting my place on *The Great Pottery Throw Down* was a big step. What finally encouraged me to sign up was that I was no longer 'Florence the Model', being judged for how I looked or who I was dating. On the show, I was 'Florence the Potter'. By then, I believed so deeply in the healing power of clay, I was ready to get stuck in and share this beautiful craft with others who love it.

⚶

It was Freya Bramble-Carter who spotted the application for new *Throw Down* contestants on Instagram and sent it over to me. At that point, I'd only been practising pottery for a few years, but I had my wheel and kiln so I'd got the basics, and I really thought I was ready. Now I realise that it takes a lifetime to master clay – but I was so utterly in love with pottery that even the thought of this challenge put fire in my belly. After I'd filled in the form there were a few long interviews over the phone. Next they asked to see me in London. There were three more interviews before they announced that I was down to the last twenty. Then came the call that I'd made it to the last ten.

I met up with all the other contestants the night before we started filming. After a train ride from London up to Stoke-on-Trent, we were booked into the accommodation that the producers provided at the local Travelodge. I had never been happier (particularly after spotting a *Love Island* contestant down the corridor!).

After checking in, it was off to dinner to meet the other potters. A few cocktails in and we were ready to stay up all night and chat about clay. But there was too much at stake, so it was early to bed, ready for the 'sparrow's fart' call at 5am.

The memory of walking onto the *Throw Down* set for the first time still sends shivers down my spine. Being back in front of the camera was never on my agenda when I took up pottery. However, part of me was ready to tell my story and show other people with depression that clay could be part of their healing too. It was pre-Covid days, so the sheer number of crew members (around 20 to 30 people) didn't bother me, but I remember being conscious that most of them were men and their constant presence at the back of the room brought familiar prickles of unease. But it was still the cameras that got to me the most. We were microphoned up in the green room just before the show, and when we entered the studio I could see how each workbench was meticulously rigged up. There was a camera suspended from the ceiling positioned right above my face, a camera on a long-extended-arm thing and a camera on the bench. Then there was this hidden Go Pro at the side of the wheel. The scrutiny was intense but this time, I was there for something I truly believed in.

Before you begin to throw off the hump, there's a moment when you tell yourself it's the right time to get stuck in; and within moments, you're away: centring the bit of clay you're working on, pressing down and then gently shaping the form, squeezing to create the curves and pinching to make the stem. Before you know it, you're cutting your creation off the hump and you're ready to go again. Everything goes quickly and you just have to get on with it. It feels like life: by putting one foot in front of the other and taking a step at a time, you'll get where you're going. But starting… well, that takes mind over matter. And that's why throwing off the hump is another perfect metaphor for me walking into the studio for *The Great Pottery Throw*

Down. It took courage for me to do that show, but once I was in the room I just had to keep digging into my inner pit of strength. When I heard that Hurricane Dorian had struck the Bahamas, I had to persevere and carry on. And when Jimmy was diagnosed with pneumonia and my natural mothering instincts kicked in, I'd had to focus on taking one step at a time. *The Great Pottery Throw Down* wasn't easy, but I managed to stay in the competition until I was shown the door in episode five. It was perfect timing; I needed to be with Jimmy. Pottery is my something, but family is my everything.

FLEA BITES

- Feel the fear but do it anyway. Going on the *Throw Down* was an enormous challenge for me, but I can now stand back and see how much good it did to share my story and to prove to myself that I could do it.

- It also helped me to shake off some of the labels I've been given. It was a brilliant opportunity to say out loud and proud, 'I am a potter!' I believe that finding your identity is a crucial part of healing from depression.

- Part of the joy of the show is watching the potters deal with cracks and smashes and bounce back from mistakes. Seeing how people cope brings hope. Months after the show had ended, I received a box of my pots by courier, but most of them had broken into pieces. I remember Iris being sad for me, but I felt calm. I don't think the old me would have reacted so well but the potter in me was quite philosophical.

7

THE EARTH BENEATH

'I think in this moment where everything is kind of
bombastic and plastic and prefabricated, that clay
feels perverse because it is lowly.'

THEASTER GATES, *THE GUARDIAN*

It's a beautiful Bahamian spring morning and I'm with my
master potter friend Doris Hamilton. She has promised that
she will show me where we can forage for clay. I've never been
foraging before. Doris is keen to pass on her knowledge and
wisdom, so we're taking a team of teenagers into the bush. 'I love
that my pots come from nothing,' she explains. 'Out of nothing,
comes something!'

This island in the Bahamas is one of many contrasts – crystal-
blue seas and mangrove swamps juxtaposed with a large industrial
port. It seems so unlikely that this rocky mass of land, with its
limestone and coral, will bear fruit, but I put my trust in Doris.

Her excitement is almost tangible. I'm buzzing too; it feels like we're off to find treasure. Clay is more precious than gold to me. We jump in the car and drive east onto the limestone flats. Out the window you can see where forest fires have ravaged the trees and the air is still thick with smoke.

Eventually we arrive at Doris's cousin's house, where we spill out of the car, giggling and laughing. Laden with shovels, pickaxes and buckets, we head into the bush, taking care to avoid any poisonwood, snakes or banana spiders along the track. Doris loves being close to nature and her breadth of knowledge is vast. She points to some mulberries – she tells us they taste better off the tree, so we stop for a nibble. Doris stops again when she sees a palm tree she recognises – apparently the palm heart found at the root is just mouth-watering, but you need to harvest it at the right time.

We carry on, with Doris leading the way. We're on the lookout for fern bushes, which grow in the shade of the pine trees. Doris tells us that the soil under the ferns is rich and contains more iron than elsewhere in the bush, so this is a good place to find clay. It's the season for forest fires, smoke swirls among the leaves and branches, and I can't help but feel a little intrepid as we march deeper into the trees. High up in the canopy, Doris sees a flash of blue, green and red and we all look up to see what looks like a rainbow bird. She tells us it's a Painted Bunting and we're lucky to spot it because it's a shy creature that usually hides amongst the foliage.

There are whoops of delight when we discover a clump of lush ferns – it's like we've found where 'X' marks the spot. The team take out their pickaxes and start chipping at the earth. The top layer is dry, eroded dirt – it doesn't look like it will yield anything at all, but we keep singing and laughing, caught up in the excitement of the moment. Next we use our shovels to dig a little deeper. The soil looks a bit grey to me, but I have faith and we keep on digging.

The earth becomes less dusty and we see a dark crust. Beneath lies a doughy, glue-like red, fertile silt. We've struck gold! Doris picks up a small handful of the iron-rich clay and crumbles it between her beautiful, weathered fingers. Rolling a ball between her palms, she looks at me with her warm, knowing smile.

———

My parents worked hard to make holidays a possibility for us when we were young. Holidays in France, and a couple of once-in-a-lifetime trips further afield, were filled with as many visits to museums and art galleries as my parents could shoehorn in. This wasn't always easy when we were very small, when our attention spans lasted ten minutes. My parents had come up with this genius idea to get us into art early, and it worked. Somehow, they managed to make art appreciation seem a central, vital part of life, regardless of one's age – it is something I am hugely grateful for, and have tried to replicate in the way I bring up my own children.

'Let's play the postcard game!' Just hearing those words transports me straight back to being a child and I feel a tingle of anticipation. My family bucked the trend for exiting the museum via the gift shop – we always *entered* through the shop. Sounds like a recipe for tantrums and meltdowns, I know. It worked because mum and dad allowed each of us to choose four postcards that depicted an artefact or work of art from one of the collections within the museum or gallery, the idea being that as we trooped around the building, we would look out for our postcard artworks. It was a bit like bingo but better – the first one to get all their postcards was declared the winner. It was competitive and we were so involved that my parents got to see what they wanted. We, without effort, were falling in love with art.

On a family holiday in Thailand, we didn't play the postcard game but I remember my mum looked out for pottery everywhere we went. We'd be driving along and she'd shout 'Pots!' every time we drove past a market stall. We'd all roll our eyes – not another bloody pot. Dad was eager to find the next pina colada and we wanted to swim. By the end of the trip, she had gathered a fabulous collection of funny old pots, including a few cookery crocks that had definitely seen better days. As the saying goes, 'one person's trash is another person's treasure'. I may laugh about it, but I know I absorbed some of her enthusiasm. I could never recreate those lovely Thai pots that she still has at home, but perhaps something about them influences my work. Potters 'borrow' ideas from each other all the time and I'm not afraid to admit that I'm a 'borrower'.

I don't need postcards to remember our first family trip to Africa. That was a really big holiday for us. We were staying with friends in the foothills of Mount Kenya, where I became fascinated with the cracks in the earth. They were all over – in the dirt roads, at the bottom of the dried-up riverbeds and in the dusty paths surrounding our friends' house. In some places, the cracks were so big it looked like there had been an earthquake. These fissures were the result of drought. During the wet season, the rain falls hard on the clay-rich soil. Clay is like a sponge – it can absorb large amounts of water. However, as it dries, the clay particles shrink and that's when the soil begins to crack. If this happens quickly, as it does under the hot African sun, the cracks can appear even more dramatic and scary.

Years later, as I make my pots, I'm very wary of the clay drying out too fast. Letting the pot dry before it is fired is part of the process: before a pot goes in the kiln it has to be 'bone dry'.

To achieve this you need warm air to encourage evaporation, combined with low humidity. Every pot is like the Kenyan land-scape – if it dries out too quickly, it will crack. In the summer, because of the heat, potters have to really keep an eye on the elements – on a dry day things can go to pot quickly (by the way, this saying doesn't come from pottery – it possibly has something to do with chopping up meat to go in the cooking pot). Even opening a door to let in a draught can make all the difference. I've learned to love the cracks. When a brittle surface splits in just the right place, it can look perfect. Well, sometimes. Cracks are part of the process in pottery, and, as we all know, in life. As the musician Leonard Cohen said, 'There is a crack, a crack in everything, that's how the light gets in.'

The soil that I encountered in Africa all those years ago had another distinctive quality. Perhaps not every ten-year-old would be into this, but I became obsessed with the variation in colours. I remember, when driving through the bush, how the earth seemed to be all yellow in one place but would suddenly become pitch black. Later down the road the soil turned a deep red. These colour changes captured my imagination.

I'd always harboured a longing to go back to Africa and, in 2022, our family was reunited under Kenyan skies to celebrate my dad's 70th birthday (albeit a year late because of Covid). I didn't miss WiFi; in fact, it was a luxury to be away from it and just listen to the sounds of the bush and the Samburu warrior songs. I had the time to really take in my surroundings and experience the earth beneath my feet.

When we pulled into a dry riverbed, mum brought out a tiny magnet and we were amazed as the grains of 'soil' were magically drawn towards it – it had to be iron ore chips – huge thrills for a potter thinking about glaze combinations. On another rest break, I unearthed large chips of obsidian (a black glass formed by volcanoes). As my fingers foraged around in the scorched soils, my head went places I never imagined – it felt like the earth was sending me a subtle reminder to sign up for a geology course pronto.

❦

I don't think there's anything more grounding and earthy than going foraging for your own clay. It usually begins with a slippery walk in wellies by a lake, stream or the seaside, or in the woods, often you don't even need to go that far because it's hiding in the soil in your back garden. You're going to get pretty mucky on your mission to extract, process and mould your wild clay, but I promise it's good fun – and it doesn't cost the earth. All you need is a bucket, a spade, a pickaxe (old and manky, it really doesn't matter), tubs for storage, lids (it feels good to recycle stuff from around the house), a turkey baster, a fine sieve, an old colander and several faded, scruffy T-shirts – some to wear and others for straining the clay. Basically, use a jumble of stuff that you were on the verge of chucking away.

Streams are among the best and easiest places to harvest clay. You'll never have to travel far to find a bubbling brook in Britain, even if you live in a city. I have often used these clay hunts to make a great day out with Iris and Jimmy. They make mudslides while I slip around delving for lovely, unctuous deposits of clay. Part of the thrill, just as when you are foraging for food, is discovering something that is in front of your very eyes. You just need to know how to look for it.

Until the summer of 2021, the closest I'd got to searching for clay in rivers (alluvial clay, if you want to be technical) was watching other potters on YouTube. This is as near to pottery ecstasy as it gets – seeing someone grab a glob of sticky mud and squeeze it to see if it holds its shape, a sure indication that you have a handful of the good stuff. I wanted in on some of that action. Alluvial clay is fascinating because the colour and consistency vary greatly according to the different minerals present in the riverbed. Going back in time, before we bought clay from a shop or had it delivered in bags through the post, streams and rivers were an easy source of clay for villagers. This is still the case in many places in the world where people use traditional pottery techniques. In Egypt, potters use Nile mud to create an array of earthy red-brown pots. The rotund clay beer pots (*ukhamba*) made by the Zulu people in parts of southern Africa get their deep dark colour from the 'black' clays foraged from the banks of the Thukela River. Raw 'black' clay is actually just a very dark grey, and to achieve that density of colour, the pots are fired twice in pits filled with smoking bark and leaves. In Africa, making pots was – and still is – considered women's work. Women collect the clay from the riverbanks and, once they have processed it (a task that takes weeks to complete), they begin coiling their pots. At the leather-hard stage, the women use pebbles or the backs of spoons to smooth and burnish the surface. Natural tools like sticks, feathers and corn cobs are used to add decoration, before animal fat or good old shoe polish is applied to give that signature high-gloss finish. 'Black' clay is also found in Oaxaca in Mexico, where it's used to make the famous Barro Negro pottery ('pottery of the night' in local folktales) – although this clay comes from the slopes of the Sierra Madre, not a riverbank.

When I was reading about the black marshes of North Carolina in Delia Owens' delicious novel *Where the Crawdads Sing*, I wondered what lay beneath them. Was it the same dark clay found on the banks of the Thukela River or in the mountains of the Sierra Madre? In the novel, the lonely and misunderstood young protagonist Kya finds solace in the natural world, making mud her mother and cure-all. Her story moved me like few others but I must admit it's the magic of the mud that has stayed with me most; I still think about following in Kya's footsteps and sinking my feet into the thick, cooling ground of those mysterious low-lying bogs and plains.

In the summer of 2021, I finally realised my dream of foraging in the UK. Biblical rainfall in August caused mayhem in parts of the countryside. Camping holidays were cut short and only the bravest and hardiest dog-walkers felt inclined to go on country walks. But when I looked out of the window at the sodden, muddy fields around my mother-in-law's Suffolk cottage, I felt this urge to pull on my wellies and go foraging. As soon as I mentioned this to the kids they jumped around with excitement. So off we set.

We made our way to one of the rivers nearby. 'Is this the right place, Mama?' Iris asked me as we reached a pretty riverbank strewn with wildflowers. This was my first time leading a foraging expedition so I wasn't sure. There was nothing for it but to start scrabbling around in the mud. But it wasn't mud – it was sand. There was no clay to be found. Perhaps the river was too uphill to be fruitful. We were all a bit disappointed and sodden wet, but the 'Ohs' soon became 'Ooohs' and 'Aaahs' as we spotted dragonflies and spied a fish in the water.

After that expedition, I was more determined than ever to find some local clay. A local friend and beekeeper brought over a tub of craggy earth and mud that he'd dug up from a claypit nearby. The kids and I were delighted and whiled away an hour in the garden squeezing and squelching it between our fingers. The mud needed to be processed, so I took a handful back home to do just that. One day, I'll make a pot with it.

If you can, find a detailed map of your local area (an old one might be even better). You may find that there are claypits or claypit forests near to you. Look for clues in place names such as Pottery Lane or Kiln Road – they often signal that pottery was made in the area, which in turn can indicate that there was clay around. It was through this trick that I discovered Claypit Spinney near Great Livermere. The clay here was used by the ancient Romans; it's stuffed with minerals from old dead fish so it should be a rich vintage. I can't wait to experiment with it one day.

If the buzz and excitement of making a pot gets you going, then actually finding your own clay will give you a natural high too. The thing that blows my mind is the sheer age of clay – it was formed millions of years ago when glaciers were shifting and sculpting the landscape. Now here I am, rolling it into a ball with my fingers. Not only that, it lasts for ever. It'll be here long after we are gone and probably outlive the plastics and other man-made materials that pollute our planet.

I feel so lucky to have grown up in a time pre-health-and-safety, with no internet, YouTube or video games to distract us.

We had to find activities to amuse ourselves. These inevitably included 'adventures' outside, building camps in the woods, making dams in the local streams and just getting our hands good and dirty in mud. I hope I'm passing a healthy respect for muck and mud on to my kids. I feel mud should be on the school curriculum. Very few schoolchildren these days will be given a lovely big lump of clay to play with, let alone be able to see it go in a kiln and undergo its magical transformation. If you were lucky enough to be given clay at school, you might recall that it always came in these uniform grey blocks. My parents still treasure the wonky thumbed pinch pots that I made as a child.

Discovering that clays come in an array of colours has been a real eye-opener for me. Most commercial studios use light-grey to white clay, but as mentioned earlier in this chapter, iron-rich clay is a deep-orange or brick colour. Darker clays may have manganese in them, the black clay of Oaxaca, for example. There's also olive-green clay, which gets its fabulous hue from a mixture of iron oxide and decomposed plant matter, seaweed and algae. Blue clay, which gets its colour from the chemically reduced (as opposed to oxidised) iron it contains, is said to have medicinal properties (it's an antibacterial and some people eat it) and it can transform to red when it's fired in the kiln. Believe it or not, there's even a purple clay. In China it's known as *zisha* and is used to make high-quality teapots.

Potters choose clays not only for their colours but also for their different properties, which make them suitable for specific purposes or to achieve a specific effect. There are three main types of pottery: earthenware, stoneware and porcelain. Terracotta is one of the most popular forms of earthenware. It's used, for example, to make flower pots, roof tiles and drainage pipes. The clay required for it is relatively easily sourced from streams, rivers, lakes and even the seaside, making it a favourite of early potters. This type of clay fires at lower temperatures (1000-1120 degrees C) and is more porous and less durable than other kinds of clay. In its moist state, it ranges from orange to red-brown to buff or grey. It has a greater plasticity and is easier to work with than most clays. The colour it takes on after firing is dependent upon the mineral content. It's a great clay for beginners and I've foraged for it in the Bahamas, Portugal and Kenya, so it has a special place in my studio. Red earthenware and white earthenware are also ideal for making slip decoration.

Stoneware clays come in a range of stony colours – greys, buffs and browns. Stoneware is stronger than earthenware so less prone to breaking. It also fires at higher temperatures and you can experiment with different heat levels (around 1200-1300 degrees C) and types of firing to create all kinds of wonderful effects. It has a hard, smooth finish and is heavier than earthenware.

Porcelain or kaolin clay is the hardest to work with, but you will be rewarded with the most tranquil whites and beautiful dove greys when it's fired. Like stoneware, porcelain requires higher temperatures (around 1280 degrees C). Lucie Rie used both stoneware and porcelain, while Edmund de Waal seems to mostly favour porcelain. I too love working with porcelain but it's very delicate and when it's bone dry it can literally crumble between your fingers, so you need to be careful when you load your creations into the kiln.

As you learn more about pottery you'll find which clay works best for you. And somewhere down the line you even might start mixing your own clay and experimenting with adding colourants. Other additives include grog, which will fortify the clay, sand, paper or even nylon. Paper clay is the most versatile and can be used to make large-scale works because it's strong. When paper clay is fired, the paper essentially burns away, leaving a honeycomb of minute holes through the clay, making it lighter. It's fabulous and fascinating to work with.

The glorious thing is that every batch of clay is unique. Sometimes when I'm kneading and wedging a lump of clay, I wonder where it came from and how it was formed. What's in the mix this time? I have been relatively lucky in life. I have a secure bedrock: a happy home and supportive family. My early relationships were loving, albeit with the usual dramas you'd expect in your teens and twenties. When did a flake of grit enter the mix? I guess the answer must be when I had PND. Fortunately, unlike clay, humans can't be defined as a certain type – we are ever-changing and evolving. But, just like clay, a flake of grit can make us stronger.

FLEA BITES

- Processing foraged clay is hard graft, but I highly recommend it. First off, you need to add water to the mud and sieve it to remove any unwanted pebbles, rocks or blades of grass. Keep repeating the sieving process over the course of a month. I usually add some stoneware slip to the mix. This isn't a must, but I love the creamy consistency that is created.

- The sieving process is quite laborious. If you have kids, try getting them involved – Jimmy loves being encouraged to make a mess while sieving.

- You may be wondering why I suggest you need a turkey baster for processing your clay. Well, during the processing, the clay settles at the bottom of the container. But there's good stuff in the watery layer that sits above this. It contains finer particles of clay and other minerals that can be extracted using the baster. Believe it or not, this slippy slime can be used as a glaze and it can create some incredible results.

- I store the foraged mud in a big old dustbin. I keep a lid on it so it doesn't dry out. In the Bahamas, a cover is a must because I'm not keen on finding any cockroach or snake remains in the mix. Having said that, they might add an interesting colour to the clay!

- Get mucky in any mud you can find. If you go mudlarking along the Thames, you may even uncover buried treasure, such as old clay pipes or even Roman coins.

- Take a mud bath. I still have to try this, but the mud baths in Dalyan in Turkey look fabulous and are definitely high on my bucket list.

- Being around or in water has always made me happy. I'm not saying you should swim in a weir with eels, but why not kick off your shoes and walk on wet grass or paddle in a stream? Experience the sensations and see how grounding yourself in nature feels.

8

SLIP, GLAZE N' SGRAFFITO

'Most mammals emerge from the womb like glazed earthenware emerging from a kiln – any attempt at remoulding will only scratch or break them. Humans emerge from the womb like molten glass from the furnace. They can be spun, stretched and shaped with a surprising degree of freedom.'

YUVAL NOAH HARARI, *SAPIENS: A BRIEF HISTORY OF HUMANKIND*

A well-formed vase sits on the plate of the pottery wheel. It's sticky wet, unturned and bottom-heavy. The turntable has only just stopped spinning but there is no pause in the process – I want to add layers of slip to this pot while it is still leather hard and I must be swift. The texture of the slip and the wet pot must mimic each other. If the slip is too wet, the pot might crack, but if it's too dry it won't stick.

I grab the coloured slip and start to paint. I start with lighter colours, so it's the yellow ochre I reach for first. It's like painting olive oil onto bread dough – soft and deeply satisfying, a thick impasto gliding across the surface.

After light comes shade. I wash my hands and run my fingers along the jars of various pigments and oxides that I have mixed with the clays to create an array of slips to dip and paint. It has taken me years to understand how these confusing metallic names will end up as colours; to discover how chemicals like copper oxide, iron oxide, cobalt carbonate and manganese dioxide transform into beautiful, rich hues when fired.

My fingers instinctively move towards the jar of celadon green – it's full of copper and will contrast nicely with the ochre (I hope). This time I choose a thick horsehair brush and, once I've dipped it in the slip, I whip it against the surface of my vase, creating a magical juxtaposition of the rough with the smooth. It's as if Jackson Pollock has tried his hand at Japanese calligraphy – dot, dot, dash, dash, squiggle, dot, dot.

I step away and study the busy surface of the pot. It's lovely. I like it as it is – but perhaps it needs more detail on its veneer. So I grab a pipette and fill it with a chocolate-brown-almost-black slip mix that I created using iron oxide. I spin the wheel gently with my left hand, as my right hand squeezes the pipette and trails the paint randomly. I want to shake off the mundanity of the day and lose myself in abstraction.

It's time to pause before I overdo it. I step away from my vase to allow it to dry a little, but I do not rest; I can always find hundreds of other things to do in the studio. After washing away the clay that's built up around my nails and fingers, I turn to my cooling kiln and busy myself with cleaning its shelves. Next I grab a handful of brushes and wash them until the water runs clear. Then comes the satisfying task of scraping clay off the bats. Chips and chunks of dry clay can spoil a new pot, so it's best to clean as you go. Tidying a kitchen is a chore, but when I sort the studio I feel immense pleasure – this is a clean-up with a bit more intention.

I return to the vase and gently tap the surface. It's no longer sticky wet but more like dried putty. I'm confident that it's time to keep pushing these layers to the limit. I want to give this pot a depth and proud beauty that can only come from layers and layers of work.

I grab my favourite carving tool, the wooden-handled sgraffito pen, which has a sharp metal nib at its head, and I begin to carve. This time I feel like I'm taking a warm knife and cutting through firm butter – it glides and sails through the surface. I'm careful not to dig too deep – I don't want any holes in this sturdy urn. I scratch, scrape and carve to reveal just a little of the colours below. The grit from the foraged clay occasionally breaks the rhythm, but I like that because it stops me in my tracks, making me pause to take account of the pot. In that space, I have time to consider where I should head next.

I'm so caught up in the process that it's tempting to carry on forever. But I decide to leave while the party is hot, before it turns into a 'full-on Monet', as actress Alicia Silverstone puts it in one of my favourite teen films *Clueless*. 'From far away, it's okay, but up close it's a big old mess.'

———

Greenware is how we describe pottery at any stage of the drying process; wet and sticky to bone dry. It's only when the clay is fully air dried and can go into the kiln to be 'bisque fired' that it transforms from greenware into bisqueware. If you tap a piece of greenware, you'll hear a quiet thud (it can sometimes crumble, so be gentle), but when the ware has been fired at least once, you'll get that joyful 'ting' that makes the heart sing.

When greenware is leather hard (before it turns bone dry), there are still plenty of opportunities for change. Perhaps you don't like the handle after all, so you can pull it off and sculpt a new one. Maybe in the few days that you've left your work under an air-tight wrap, you change your mind and want to tweak it. You can. This is basically the final edit for your piece of greenware, before you

get going with slip, sgraffito or glaze. If your piece is hand-built, slabbed or coiled, the skeleton shape is now ready and this is your opportunity to add texture and decoration. If your pot is thrown on the wheel, there's still one more step before decoration: turning. Turning is when you can transform a rough-hewn, lumpy old pot into a sculpted, refined thing of beauty. Some people describe this stage as trimming or shaving, and there are lots of implements you can use to help you along: the loop tool for turning, the nifty craft knife for slicing and cutting, the spatula for shaving, the kidney and rib for smoothing, or a mud-shredder, which is shaped like a cheese grater and refines the surface of your pot. Maybe you need to trim away parts of the walls to make them even, or just to neaten everything up. Perhaps you want to create a foot or add a rim.

When I started out in pottery, there were some processes that I loved immediately and others that felt like a chore. One of the latter was turning pots, bowls and vases on the wheel. This was the stage when things seemed to go wrong: plates would fly off the wheel or I'd apply too much wet clay and they'd stick to the bottom. Maybe one side of my pot was too brittle and had dried out too much compared with the other side – or I'd find a hairline fracture when it was eventually fired to bisque.

I now realise that it's actually a very exciting phase, which can literally make or break a pot. This is the time when you have to take full advantage of the moisture stage of your greenware if, for example, you want to create a beautiful and consistent pot with a good base. Too wet, and the walls wobble and flop inwards and collapse, or you make an annoying hole. Too dry, and you'll end up with clouds of dust in your face. If this happens, stop immediately because it's dangerous for your lungs to be breathing in this very fine dust.

When you're shaving a pot, the clay should peel away like ribbons – like shavings of the soul. I've grown to love this process and find it hugely satisfying. So much so that I have to watch myself: when I get going with a loop tool and begin scraping away those long plumes of clay, it's easy to get carried away and sabotage the pot.

Always remember: the joy of greenware is that, unlike bisqued clay, it can be recycled back into slip and then wedged into shape again. If your masterpiece isn't quite up to scratch, take a strong tool like a rolling pin or even a hammer and simply smash it up. This is a great exercise in not getting too attached and it's wonderful to chuck your creation into the clay recycling bin and watch as the water gobbles it up. Wouldn't it be great if we could sling all our bad experiences into a recycling pot and let them submerge, never to be seen again? Life isn't like that, of course. Our mistakes and the bad things that happen to us have a way of bubbling to the surface from time to time. But that isn't necessarily a bad thing. When stuff gets tough, those recycled chunks of life experience help us to get through the next stage.

¢

I have talked a lot in this book about the joys of working and playing with clay, of being anchored by this earthy, life-enhancing material while at the same time transported by it. One of the most important lessons I've learned as a potter is knowing when to put down the tools. I like to have a vision of what I'm going to make before I set foot in the studio, but sometimes, when I'm lost in a pot, I just keep playing because it's interesting to see where it may lead. I've lost a few greenware beauties this way and many more at the slip and glazing stages. I try to listen to my inner voice. Only then can I get a feel for when I should let my instinct take me further into my art, and when I should pull back and stop.

Obviously, it's hard to listen to *all* the voices in your head – creative whispers and those pleas to stop can often cancel each other out. Grayson Perry has clearly found a happy medium – his ceramics can get very busy, but he always strikes the right balance when transforming the pain felt from childhood or the angst of the modern world into scenes on the outside of his pots.

Decoration is such a thrilling stage of the process and there are so many varieties of juicy slips, bright underglazes, metallic oxides and scintillating glazes to choose from. The first thing to know is that, while slip and glaze are both decorative techniques, slip is usually applied to greenware and glazing once the pot has been bisque fired. Slip is essentially sieved, broken-down, wet, liquid clay, which adds texture, colour and layers to greenware. It is also used for slip casting, a process involving pouring liquid clay into a mould and allowing it to set and solidify. A slightly thicker consistency is required for slip trailing (see Glossary).

Generally speaking, it's better to apply a decorative slip when the clay is damp, before it becomes leather hard, and definitely before it's bone dry. It can take greenware pottery anything up to seven days to become bone dry, but by then it's too late to get busy with slips and tools. A bone-dry pot feels warmer and lighter

because it's lost all its moisture. It's super-brittle and vulnerable, so you don't want to handle it except to put it in the kiln to be bisque fired. When that moment comes, you have to go carefully.

Have you ever seen those ancient Greek pots with black or red decoration in the British Museum? They are some of the earliest Western examples of slip decoration. In Britain, the best early slips were created by potters in seventeenth-century Staffordshire and Kent. Ceramicists have been refining and playing with the process ever since – and that includes me and most of the potters I know.

It's pretty easy to make your own slip. Simply take a bag of bone-dry clay and bash it with a hammer until it's reduced to small chips. This really gets the blood pumping. Then crush the chips with a rolling pin to get a fine clay powder, a process which is also hugely soothing and satisfying. After this, you decant the clay powder into a jar (wearing a mask to avoid inhaling the dust) and add water. Afterwards, you can blitz the mix in a blender or stir it up by hand. Thicker slips are useful as glue or filler for when you're building your pots – again it's surprisingly therapeutic to squish and squelch this mish-mash between your fingers.

Decorating slips, which are thinner and less sticky, need a bit more water added and, of course, colour pigments. I have drawers full of natural pigments – once you get into buying them it's hard not to get carried away. You can buy ready-mixed coloured slips too but I prefer DIY. If you store your precious creations with a tight lid, they will last you ages and best of all, cost you very little in the long run. And always remember to wear an apron when you're dealing with them. The other day, I was adding water to a slip that had dried up a bit and I forgot to screw the lid on tightly. A fountain of slip gushed over Jimmy, who'd been working with me in the studio that day. Luckily it wasn't an oxide, or it would have stained. And fortunately again, it was just a porcelain slip and non-toxic. Jimmy and I shared one of those delicious belly-laughing moments. There was no crying over spilt slip.

Adding colour to slip is when the amateur scientist in me comes out to play. Squint your eyes and look at the shelves of coloured slips in my studio and you could easily mistake them for chemicals lined up in a laboratory. My hotchpotch of pots, mostly recycled jam and olive jars, contain luscious shades that I've created using pigments I've bought from art shops or online – you can buy them in every colour of the rainbow. Each slip mix I make is about 5 per cent pigment, the rest being clay and water. I usually use an old kitchen whisk to mix mine but I do see other potters swooshing the ingredients together with their hands. On the whole, I find that you can be a little more random and experimental with slip recipes than with those for glaze, which need to be very scientific and precise.

I tend to mix my own slips at the beginning of the kids' new school term. It's a way of embracing that 'back to class' feeling, preparing enough to see me through the next few months. I think perhaps this gives my work a sense of time and place – in the same way that fashion has seasons and changing colours, pottery trends can be inspired by the mood and weather.

I'm useless at labelling my jars, so there are a fair few slip mixes hanging around on my shelves that are a complete mystery to me. The day I decide to use those slips is going to be very interesting. I wonder whether Robert Picault, one of my favourite ceramicists, had the same problem. Picault was a neighbour and collaborator of Picasso's when they both resided in Vallauris in the South of France after the Second World War. He was a master of hand decoration and was part of a revival of the art in the 1950s. Picasso and Picault became friends, and I can easily imagine the pair of them discussing their work over a few glasses of wine in the afternoon sun, then heading back to the studio where Picault would get his slips in a mix and forget to label them like I do. Whatever those two were up to, I love the vibrancy of Picault's work; his funky plates and bold homewares wouldn't look out of place in any kitchen now. He has become quite collectable – you can find his pieces on Etsy and eBay. If you're tempted, especially if you're lucky enough to find one in a charity shop or flea market, make sure it has his

'RP' maker's mark on the bottom before you fork out too much. Even if you have a shrewd eye, it's easy to be fooled by a fake. I was delighted to unearth a few of his treasures at a brocante in Avignon, France. You often find dodgy replicas when you go trawling through these flea markets, but you may find gems if you look hard enough.

The rustic simplicity of Picault's work gets me excited. I love inspecting the layers of craftsmanship that have gone into each piece. He often used terracotta clay topped with a pink or white tin glaze, layered with copper oxide patterns. The copper oxide against the pink glaze perhaps inspired Lucie Rie to choose this combination in the 1970s. I so admire the way that the pinks and greens somehow clash and harmonise at the same time.

Sgrafitto is one of my favourite decorative techniques. After applying various layers of slip to the pot's surface, I use a sharp instrument to sgraffito a line drawing through the slip layers. The subtlety of the colour is further enhanced after the pot has been bisque fired, and the results can be very powerful. Sgrafitto tools and instruments come in all shapes and sizes – you can use pencils, crayons or anything with a point. I like to use a Bic pen because it produces a lovely smooth line. Lots of potters use the sgraffito stage to create interesting colour contrasts. I'm naturally drawn to organic colours, so again, I turn to the great Lucie Rie for inspiration; she seemed to have fun with full-on colour while also achieving some triumphant results with rawer volcanic glazes.

Every piece of pottery has a tale to tell, so I always inspect ceramics with respect. The artist adds layer upon layer – some of these will have been intentional but others may easily have been mistakes. One of the most intriguing contemporary potters I've discovered recently is Janet Haig. I remember seeing her pottery on display in a clothes shop in London in my twenties and being blown away. Those earthy pots mystified me – how did she create all those coats, surfaces and textures and produce such an extraordinary veneer? The pots were coiled, but there were holes and other marks that she had added or scraped away that defy description. It was hard to uncover all her secrets, but whatever techniques Janet had used, those pots made a deep impression on me.

Delving further into Janet Haig's life has only strengthened my belief that a potter's spirit is unleashed not only in the form of their creations but in those layers of slip, sgraffito and glaze. Janet says it's amazing how your early life affects what comes later on.[18] You can see that mirrored in her unique pots, which have been a work in progress since her childhood in Poland during the Second World War. Janet was wrenched apart from her father and baby sister to live in a Siberian prison with her mother. She was young, so her mother took along a little blue enamel pot for warming her daughter's meals – it was one of the few possessions they managed to keep and Janet still has it today. Is that blue pot the inspiration for the shades of blue that adorn the surface of many of Janet's creations? Janet lost most of her family during the war; she believes her father was shot and the rest were killed at Treblinka. Loss like this leaves deep scars – and I search for these in her pots. Maybe that's her intention; she chooses not to use glaze because it would cover those marks. Rather, she works with natural materials – like an oxide or pigment – to create colour, which she gently brushes on like a painter.

After the war, Janet studied art in Australia, and says that she has always been inspired by nature, wherever she has been in the world. In some of her plates, I feel I can almost see the burnt Australian outback against the hot sky.

Janet believes that clay has a life of its own and there is no certainty about how things will evolve. I wonder if she used her art to absorb her life experiences. Given the many hardships she suffered, it would have been so easy to succumb to depression, but whenever she needed an outlet she turned to drawing, painting and more recently ceramics and sculpture. 'I hope to be like Lucie Rie and go on until I'm 90,' she says.

Like so many potters, Janet collects stones, bits of wood, cones and other natural objects. On my travels I have collected acacia beeswax to polish a burnished surface, palm seeds for decoration and, of course, soil and stones for making and glazing – because these collected items inspire the way I want to shape things and help me to conjure the colours I want to achieve. Most of us are on a constant mission to discover new things and unravel secrets – all the better if they're from nature. Michel Francois, an amazing master potter I know, forages for clay along the coast where he lives in Cornwall, and even likes to gather granite dust from the local quarry for his glazes, somehow transforming all this grit, gravel and fresh earth into the most stunning, curvaceous feminine forms.

Potters are a generous bunch, but when it comes to glaze recipes, we can be rather tight-lipped. Imagine if you discovered something magical and unique, wouldn't you feel protective? Especially as it can take years of experimenting to find the right mix for a colour or an effect you want to achieve, and sometimes you have to experiment over and over to get the effect you want. In the eighteenth century, apparently the European potteries were secretive about their recipes too – especially for golden gilding, where the addition of something as simple as old vinegar could make all the difference to the final shimmering look.

These days I keep a little diary with recipes for my own glazes. I record the compounds and minerals that are required. So for my volcanic glaze, the one that bubbles and makes exciting indentations, I have noted down the components, which happen to be silica, flint, whiting, custer feldspar, Edgar Plastic Kaolin, titanium dioxide and silicon carbide – all of which sound straight out of a laboratory.

If you ever tuned into *The Great Pottery Throw Down* in 2020, you may remember an Irish girl with a massive smile – that's my friend Claire Murdock. In the first episode, she blew us all away with her exquisite breakfast set, which demonstrated her fearless use of black iron oxide added to her white dipping glaze. The mesmerising gradient of colour that she achieved brought tears to the eyes of Keith Brymer Jones, and deeply impressed the rest of us. Claire and I have kept in contact since the show and whenever I have questions about glazes, I give her a call so we can talk potter to potter. Claire is very generous with her extensive knowledge of recipes so, if I want a shiny blue glaze, I'll tell her what I have on my shelves and hope she has the formula. I have a hunch it needs china porcelain, titanium dioxide and maybe another oxide but I'm not totally sure. In ten seconds flat, Claire comes up with the exact recipe with the percentages I need. She's the ultimate 'phone a friend'.

Making glazes is a science. Because I'm not a natural scientist, this is part of the pottery journey that I've had to work hard on. But equally, I've not allowed myself to get too hung up on it. I'd advise anyone to get to know four or five pigment and oxide combinations really well. Learn the base ingredients of a glaze – silica (sand), which is the glass-forming ingredient, aluminium oxide which is the stiffening agent and a flux, which causes the mixture to fuse – and then start experimenting with effects. Or as Picasso said, 'learn the rules like a pro, so you can break them like an artist.' I think this is where making glazes becomes more like cooking. By adding a pinch of this or a flake of that, you may just hit upon the magic recipe. Of course, it's handy if you've noted everything you've done so you can replicate this wizardry. As the cook and writer Nigel Slater states, 'You can make the same recipes you know over and over again, and it's different every time. I know from talking to potters, it's the same with pots.'[19] I'd second this – pops and bubbles, dribbles and drops of glaze can go wayward in the kiln. It's a transformative process and anything can happen to those layers of decoration. Glazing is also the final step so there's something special about these finishing touches.

To confuse matters more, Lucie Rie did not follow the usual procedure of bisque firing, applying glaze and re-firing it. She would sometimes apply the glaze directly to greenware and then fire the piece only once. Perhaps this single firing is the reason why she achieved such bold colour contrasts. I hope this encourages you to experiment to your heart's content. Over the years, I've found myself playing with Rie's technique. Recently I made some deep-dusky-pink-glazed miso bowls. I painted the edges with a commercial copper glaze, then simply scored into the edges with my sgraffito pen at the greenware stage. The bowls were totally inspired by Rie and I loved them. It was a real struggle to pack them up and send them off to a client in Australia. They were one of a kind and I made sure to take a photo for my memory bank (and Instagram) before I sent them on their way.

During lockdown, I made a ceramic lamp with Iris. We began by making the base – really just a large vase – on the wheel. Then I covered it with a lovely combination of orange and brown slip, by which time, Iris was desperate to do her bit, so I handed her a pencil to use as a sgraffito tool. That's when my little apprentice just went sgraffito crazy. I stood back and watched her do what she wanted. It was a beautiful moment – like I'd passed on the baton (a tool in this case) and allowed her to take charge. At the same time, I felt this analogy between my pots and parenting. Many potters express how their pottery feels like a child. And here I was with my flesh-and-blood child who was embellishing my pot. The pot was yet to be glazed or fired, so it was still a work in progress, but there was Iris making her mark. Just watching her unleash her own creativity on my creation caused a curious mix of emotions – we were in this together, but at the same time she was going her own way. It also felt like I'd come full circle – the fear I had had when she was a baby, that terrifying feeling of being a mother when I had PND, had gone.

Now I love being a mother and, aside from pottery, I feel my family is what defines me. I felt the same whoosh of emotions when I took the lamp base out of the kiln to inspect its beauty. Sometimes I have echoes of that feeling when I switch on that very lamp. The circuit is complete, the light goes on.

FLEA BITES

- It's best to turn and trim a pot when the clay is leather hard. This is the point at which the clay is neither brittle and super-fragile, nor too hard to transform. Change is something we can achieve throughout our lives, but it's easier if we're not set in our ways or too vulnerable to turn ourselves around.

- You need to put in the groundwork when it comes to adding layers to a pot. Make sure your pot is as smooth as you can make it. Mix the slips in advance. Keep a clean studio so nothing sticks to the new pot that you're creating – it will help you to breathe easier too. Plan ahead and take your time to get the best results. Be bold with decorative tech-niques when it feels right and don't be scared to experiment. Hone your knowledge of when to stop. You can apply all these rules to living your #best life too, including not saying 'yes' to everything.

- I have scratched the surface of decorative techniques in this chapter. Slip, sgraffito and glazing are my favourite ways to adorn the walls of my pots, but there are plenty of other methods and experiments to explore. Stamping, sprigging, piercing, burnishing and banding are just some of the examples of the ways you can decorate your pots. You can also try applying your glazes by spraying, flicking and dipping, as well as simply painting them on.

- Keeping a record of your glaze ingredients and combinations in a notebook is helpful. I also keep the actual test tiles as a physical reminder of the decorative techniques that work (and the ones that don't).

- Writing is also a great way of discovering more about yourself. The sculptor Barbara Hepworth regularly wrote in her journal about her family, relationships, work and travels. It's interesting to see how she juggled it all and how aspects of her life influenced her art. You may find that writing is therapeutic for you, too. It might even give you inspiration for your own creations.

9

INTO THE FIRE:
THE BEAUTY OF
IMPERFECTION

'In one and the same fire, clay grows hard and
wax melts.'

FRANCIS BACON

I feel like a little girl again. Freya Bramble-Carter and I have been digging in the sand and beachcombing all day. We're pretty proud of the hole we've dug – it's deep enough to swallow up the pile of pots that we've been making on the wheel on the beach all week.

This is no ordinary hole. It's a fire pit and I've been planning this for well over a year. Freya and her sister Yolanda are staying with us so it's the perfect opportunity to fire some pots. Freya has done this before on *The Great Pottery Throw Down*, but I'm relatively new to it and excited about what will happen. Pit firing is magical – like wizardry, or alchemy. However you'd like to think of it, it's just bloody amazing and the whole event feels like a beach party.

We have followed instructions about how to construct the pit. First of all, we lined it with stones and pebbles from the beach. Next we poured in wood shavings. Then came the fun bit as we prepared our bisqued pots for the fire. It's a bit like a fashion show – each pot gets its own makeover. Some have been stuffed with banana peels, which can create greens and greys. Others have been bound with copper wire, which leaves streaks of green, blue and reddish maroon on the surface. Crinkly bits of black seaweed, wisps of our own hair and just about any interesting bits and bobs from the beach are adorning our parade of pots.

Dusk is approaching and it feels like the witching hour cometh. The air is fizzing with anticipation. Right now we have to work quickly, because as soon as night falls on this beach, it will be pitch black. We carefully bed our precious pots into the layer of wood shavings. At this point, some potters scatter oxides or powdered glazes on top – these develop in the flames, creating a wild and wonderful spectrum of colours on the pots. Others use natural colourants like shells, nutshells, dried coffee grounds, fruit peel, leaves, pet fur or horsehair. This is an ancient practice and it does seem as if absolutely anything goes – each and everything leaves its unique signature once it's combined with fire.

Finally, we pile more leaves, sticks and logs on top of the pyre. We set it alight and watch as the fire takes hold and begins to eat away at everything on the stack. By now it's dark. We've been joined by friends and family and there's music. Iris and Jimmy are excited because there are marshmallows to toast over the fire. It crackles and their little faces glow and appear bewitched by the dancing flames.

There's no moon tonight but the stars are twinkling brightly. The sound of the waves gently crashing on the shoreline is ever present, a reminder that this magic requires all the elements – earth, fire and water.

Of course, it's more than magic – it's science too. Luckily, there's a newcomer on the island to guide us through the process. Joe is a scientist working at a coral farm called Coral Vita, which is helping protect the world's dying coral reefs. As he stokes the fire, he explains how the flames need to reach a certain temperature for the chemicals to combust, change composition and attach themselves to our wares. My mind leaps forward to tomorrow. What will our pots look like in the morning? The left and right side of my brain are on fire and I'm burning with expectation...

Until that blazing night, most of my firing had taken place in a simple electric kiln. A kiln is really just an oven but one with the ability to reach temperatures of over 1200 degrees C. To give you an idea of how hot that is, it takes just 180 degrees to roast a chicken. If you join a local pottery studio, you're more likely to find an electric kiln there because they are safer and easier to use than other kinds. An electric kiln is an ideal choice for anyone who feels ready to take their pottery journey a little further – they come in a range of sizes and specifications. When I first started, I wanted something small to fit in my kitchen, but perhaps you have a garage or a dedicated studio, which can accommodate something larger. Luckily, there's a kiln for every space. Potters are constantly trading up for bigger, better kilns so you might get a good deal second hand.

Once you've been into pottery for a while, the world of kilns opens up to reveal many possibilities. There are all kinds to choose from, including wood, oil, coal or gas fired. I'd love to try them all out one day. In his book, *Boy in a China Shop*, Keith Brymer Jones gives a vivid account of the oil-fired kiln he used as an apprentice: 'It was a right Frankenstein's monster piece of machinery, custom-built by Robert and Alan [his bosses] to their own specifications. They had integrated two old funeral burners to power the kiln and they were mightily effective. It was 250 cubic feet and could easily accommodate 1,500 mugs at a time.'[20]

Industrial Portuguese kilns are even bigger than this, about the size of a small car.

Most electric kilns are comparatively straightforward beasts; that are either top-loading or front-loading (a bit like washing machines or fridges respectively). Inside, the metal casing is lined on all sides with insulating firebricks, into which the elements are placed. There is also kiln furniture for stacking – so shelves, props, cranks and stilts. If you have a front-loader then you must mean business – they usually take up more space but they're easier to load and last longer so they make sense if you're running a commercial venture. I love the story that David Attenborough tells about Lucie Rie, who clearly had a top-loader – apparently on the day he was interviewing her at her studio he had to grab her feet to stop her falling into her kiln. Another Lucie Rie story I enjoy is how she acquired that famous raw-glazed style that I mentioned before. It went back to her days in Vienna, before she owned a kiln. She had to travel across the city with her unfired pots, a dangerous journey that she was only prepared to make once in case they broke. As a result, she pared down the process and would fire the pots straight to stoneware temperature, skipping the bisque stage and the extra trip to the kiln that this would need. A happy accident.

I'm sure lots of potters name their kilns – I called my first 'the Little Green Monster'. Even though it was only about the size of a microwave, it was a fabulous fiery thing which liberated me from the communal studio and allowed me to be adventurous in my own space. I ordered in some clay and began coiling and pinching all the plates, cups and vases and then tried firing them at different temperatures. Sometimes I added speckles of gold lustre or tried out another glaze I'd bought online and just tested, tested and tested until I got the effect I was looking for.

My absolute dream of a kiln would be the front-loading Rhoder, but for one of these you're looking at the price of a car. As I get older, rather than hankering for jewellery and clothes, I just lust after the next best kiln or wheel. For now, I'm very happy with my top-loading Viking kiln by Paragon. It was the biggest I could afford but when I installed it, I ran into a surprising problem. I hadn't realised how tall the kiln was and I couldn't reach deep inside! I soon sorted this with a small step. I hope I never do a Lucie Rie and fall in.

At first, I don't think I fully appreciated the skills involved in packing a kiln. When you're part of a communal studio, you leave your pots on the side to be fired and when you come back the next week, they are finished – 'just like that'. When you're running your own kiln, because it costs a lot, you really want to maximise the number of pots you fit inside. So the game begins: you have to try to fit them snuggly in, while ensuring, at the glazing stage particularly, that they don't touch and fuse together in the heat. You also have to ensure that every pot is in the right place for the effect you'd like to achieve. I have the utmost respect for Chris Bramble's expert arranging skills and recently had to call him for advice because some of my pots were sticking to the bottom of the kiln. Chris recommended using batt wash, a product that protects the kiln's shelves from deposits of glaze. It seems crazy that I hadn't heard of this before, but you learn something new every day with pottery – usually from another potter friend. Most recently, Gregory Tingay suggested small bisque discs as another way of preventing disasters caused by runny glaze – you place the pot on a small round disc of bisque clay, like a little mat, so that if the glaze does run, the kiln shelf is preserved.

One of my great guilty pleasures is watching Florian Gadsby (whom I mentioned in Chapter 4) as he goes about his meticulous procedures packing his kiln. His videos make compulsive viewing – check him out on YouTube as he jigsaws together shelves, stacks, props and pots. Lucky Florian has a front-loader, so I watch with curiosity, as sometimes it takes him a couple of hours to fit everything in; it's fascinating seeing how he does it and I'm not the only one watching – he has nearly 900,000 subscribers. Something of Florian's machine-like prowess must be rubbing off on me because these days, I'm much more fastidious about packing my own kiln.

As time goes by, I've got to know my kiln very well and I understand that it can do millions of magical things that I haven't even discovered yet. It's a matter of experimentation – so, for example, you can test the same glaze at ten different temperatures, and you can raise and lower the temperatures at different speeds too. I feel like I am very much a novice in this department and still just scratching at the surface, but once again, the excitement of knowing there's more to learn is thrilling. The variables are incredible and it's a whole new science, which I'll be playing with forever more.

Tinkering around with my kiln has brought out another side in me too – the practical handywoman. During lockdown, I managed to fix it myself. For a while, I'd been setting the kiln to 1260 degrees C, but the glazes weren't melting. What was going on? It kept happening over and over until at last I realised that there must be something wrong with the elements. I ordered some new elements online, but because I was living on an island, I couldn't just call in a kiln engineer to fit them; I had to step into that role and refit them myself. Luckily, Joe, our friend from Coral Vita, and a sort of walking science encyclopaedia, was around on the day that I chose to get to work. I had forgotten to unplug the kiln before I got out the toolbox, and he stopped me just before I took a screwdriver to it. That was another lesson learned and thankfully electrocution was avoided. I think the

whole experience of fixing the kiln myself gave me a new-found confidence. Another high-five for clay and a big thumbs-up for stepping into the fire.

&

As you get deeper into clay, you may find yourself reaching for some unusual bedtime reading. For a long time, I became obsessed with different ways of firing and I'd curl up with my copy of *Alternative Kilns and Firing Techniques* by James C. Watkins and Paul Andrew Wandless and fantasise about combustibles.[21] Most of the techniques they talked about were risky, with in-your-face flames and the high possibility of exploding pots and definitely some eyebrow singeing. The incredible results looked worth it. It gave me ideas about trailing horsehair, ears of corn or feathers on the outside of the fired pots to create beautiful effects.

One of the most dangerous and dramatic firing processes is the ancient Japanese art of raku, which involves glazing pieces at very high temperatures for a short time in a small specialist kiln, before removing them while red-hot – a perilous task given you're using tongs while wearing goggles and gloves – and then either plunging them into cold water (cue lots of fizzling) or covering them in combustibles which sizzle and smoke and leave behind an imprint. The contestants tried raku in one of the early series of *The Great Pottery Throw Down*, and I was desperate to give it a go. I watched as they placed their pots in chambers of feathers, oak sawdust, gorse, seaweed and even manure. The results were fabulous – mysterious squiggles and organic impressions. So you can imagine my excitement when we were told during the filming of the 2019 series that we too would be doing raku. Our task was to hand-build two animal figurines. My natural style is to make thin, delicate walls, but we had to build something that could handle the thermal shock. So my mother and baby dove were much clunkier and lumpier than I'd usually make, but they survived the blaze and I was pleased with them.

Sadly, I never got to experiment in the firepit on the show because I was knocked out before that episode. I loved the idea of going camping with the team and having a few more G and Ts in the great outdoors. I imagined sitting around the fire swapping tales and pottery secrets. Pit firing is so different from firing in a kiln – it feels feral and free and you never know how it's going to turn out.

My first pit-firing attempt was in a dustbin in my backyard in London when the kids were tiny. I'm pretty resourceful and if pushed can get handy with a drill, which I used to make holes in the metal bin. Plus, I love getting dirty and don't mind getting my fingers burned if it means discovering something new. Our garden was small, so there wasn't much room for manoeuvre. It started well – orange flames making satisfying crackling sounds as they ate up the firewood in my makeshift pit. Very soon, my garden was filled with delicious wafts of wood smoke – a smell that reminds me of bonfires in autumn and cosy fires at Christmas. It was idyllic for about two minutes, but then black smoke began pouring from the drilled holes and from underneath the rim of the rickety old lid. 'Oh f**k.' Our easy grass was starting to melt and I was beginning to panic; my little experiment was about to get totally out of hand. What would the neighbours think? The smoke hit the back of my throat and my heart was racing. The flutters and the f**ks were getting pretty furious by the time I dashed indoors to get water. I still remember the relief as I doused the flames out. There was another lesson here: possibly something about not stepping into the fire until you're ready?

Years later, the time felt right to revisit the firepit idea. This time we were in the Bahamas and there was a beach at our fingertips – billows of smoke were not going to bother our neighbours this time. In fact, everybody seemed very excited about a bonfire and I was lucky that Freya was around to join in with this particular adventure in pottery. Once the flames died down to embers, I looked around and felt a real feeling of togetherness with everyone there. By then, the children were rubbing their eyes and battling sleep, so we carried them home to bed.

I slept like a baby that night and we all woke early so we

could dash back to the firepit and retrieve our pots. Dressed in our pyjamas, we sifted through the sand and ashes, as if we were on some kind of archaeological dig. We all had very different expectations of what we would find. My sister-in-law Fatima was keen to know exactly what the pots would look like from the very start – she was keen to understand the precise science. Freya and Yolanda understood the process and were happy to let the magic happen and see where it went. Meanwhile, I had put so much time and effort into preparing the pots that I was concerned about how they had turned out. Would they have survived?

A few pots came out whole, but lots were in pieces and they had a strange beauty about them. Our cache of unglazed pots had been transformed into mystifying works of art with smudges of black, whispers of copper and shades born of the sea. It was yet another lesson in life and pots. Sometimes things don't work out exactly as you planned, but you have a choice about how you deal with the outcome – perhaps there is beauty within the broken bit and you just have to look a little harder to see it. And there's always the next time – I've made countless mistakes, especially when trying something new. But I'm discovering that those mistakes can be the makings of something even more wonderful.

Firing can seem like judgement day in pottery, the make-or-break moment when all is won or lost. I remember one particular porcelain shell, which I was so excited about, and being thrilled to see it had survived the not-quite-so-hot-as-it-should-be temperature of the kiln and transformed into this glorious sculpture. Then came the 'CRACK' as the cold air hit the surface. So yes, I know full well how the vagaries of the kiln can provide frustration, disappointment, heartbreak… But also excitement – what a wonderful metaphor for life the kiln makes. I've extracted cracked crocks off the blocks, sighed over pock-marked pots and cursed sticky bottoms. But, all of these cockups are worth it for the delight and wonder when I open my kiln and I'm bowled over by a real beauty. I'll always feel like a child on Christmas Eve when I draw back the lid, but with experience I've become a little more philosophical about the mistakes.

I think that one of the greatest hurdles with depression is acceptance of the self, but with time and clay, I'm learning to love my scars because they make me who I am now. Life is never going to be perfect and I'm not always going to be the ultimate mother, wife, or person. I forgive myself these days. If I hadn't been so ill – so broken – then maybe I wouldn't have reached for clay at all. Pottery has been a reconnection to the light and love in my world. It's given me routine, a framework for thinking and taken me on a thrilling journey into my creativity. Clay has helped me in many ways, but perhaps the biggest gift is that it's helped me reach an understanding of the real me, cracks and all.

'Pull yourself together.' How many times has that phrase

been said to somebody going through depression? I know I've heard it. But when you're dealing with the double whammy of depression and anxiety, you just don't think it's possible 'to get your act together'. People may say you look fine but inside you feel broken. Matt Haig describes this brilliantly in his book, *Reasons to Stay Alive*: 'From the outside a person sees your physical form, sees that you are a unified mass of atoms and cells. Yet inside you feel like a Big Bang has happened. You feel lost, disintegrated, spread across the universe amid infinite dark space.'[22]

PND has a cruel way of twisting the knife because not only are you depressed but you feel this insane darkness when you're supposed to feel full of light and joy. How is it possible to feel that way when you have a beautiful new baby to cherish? Well, I did. And that's where the guilt crept in. I did get over PND, but the guilt stuck around – nobody can see it but it's there, an invisible crack that will never go away but smoothes with time.

Wabi-sabi is a Japanese approach towards living which has become very popular. It focuses on finding beauty within the imperfections of life and accepting the natural cycle of decay, growth and change. In other words, accepting your flaws and working with them rather than against them – in a funny way I did this with my porcelain shell when I found beauty in the crack. Kintsugi, or 'joining with gold', is a centuries-old art of repair which comes from a similar school of thought, and, which, for the Japanese, is part of a broader philosophy of embracing the beauty of imperfection – it's about filling the gaps in an artful way. The Japanese have been mending broken pots and preserving pottery by filling the cracks with lead and gold for over 500 years. Skilled craftsmen painstakingly repair bowls with little attempt to hide the breaks – fractures filled with gold lacquer are made beautiful again, perhaps even more so, and the pot can be used and cherished by future generations.

The potter Edmund de Waal turned to this ancient process to breathe life and meaning into the pottery he created during the Covid lockdowns. He used the technique as 'a way of marking loss', in response to the devastating effects of the pandemic. Kintsugi-inspired pottery has also caught on commercially in recent years; you can buy anything from plant pots to cereal bowls with manufactured cracks made pleasing to the eye. However, I appreciate the real thing: when something that was deemed almost worthless has been repaired its sentimental value becomes greater than its monetary worth. If you hold a kintsugi pot in your hand, you can see its history, you can feel the cracks and indentations but also sense the love and care that made it whole again.

On our recent family trip to Africa, I made a selection of pots for my brother, sisters and parents to decorate with anything they could find in the African bush. Everybody went for it; splatters of camel pee and sprinklings of buffalo hair were just a few ingredients. There was one particular pot that we fired together that just couldn't stand the heat – it shattered into pieces in the fire. But I didn't want to give up on it and so I brought the pieces home, ordered some kintsugi glue and stayed up late one night sticking them back together. That pot will always remind me of this special time when we came together over Easter 2022 and healed as a family – we quite literally bonded under African skies.

Another inspiring book that calls upon us to start afresh every morning and learn from the experiences and the chance encounters we have that day is *Everyday Sacred: A Woman's Journey Home* by Sue Bender. At the end of the book, Sue recounts her experience of kintsugi and raku firing, and sets herself the task of breaking one of her unglazed bowls. She found this difficult and couldn't let go. She explains how she kept on trying but smashing things up wasn't something she was used to. On her fifth attempt, she finally cracked the bowl. 'The effect of the bowl cracking was visceral,' she writes. 'I took a long deep breath, feeling great relief – a release.' The pieces were later fired in a metal bucket filled with wood chips – I can almost picture the heat and smoke. She describes the deep satisfaction she felt later, when she glued the first two pieces back together: 'I felt I was holding a baby in my arms – just holding, with such a quiet tenderness, doing a task and being still at the same time. "All of me" was present.' [23]

This takes me back to Bernard Leach and one of the stories he recounts from ancient China: 'In one of them a noble is riding through the town and he passes a potter. He admires the pots the man is making: their grace and a kind of rude strength in them. He dismounts from his horse and speaks with the potter. "How are you able to form these vessels so that they possess such convincing beauty?" "Oh," answers the potter, "you are looking at the mere outward shape. What I am forming lies within. I am interested only in what remains after the pot is broken.'"

FLEA BITES

- As we built our firepit on the beach, we were mindful to position the sticks and stones so there was space for the air to flow. This helps the fire to burn and achieve the heat required to fire a pot. I like this idea when I think about relationships – oxygen feeds the flame and air allows love to grow. As Khalil Gibran says in *The Prophet*, 'Let there be spaces in your togetherness, and let the winds of the heavens dance between you. Love one another but make not a bond of love: let it rather be a moving sea between the shores of your souls.'[24] Henry and I chose this passage for our wedding.

- Firepits – some people have them in the garden for barbecuing or for warmth on a chilly night. I now look at them and think about how good they'd be for firing pots. I have the same thoughts when I look at pizza ovens, grills or anything that heats up – what are the possibilities for pottery? Adam, a fellow contestant from *The Great Pottery Throw Down*, is perfecting micro-raku – now that's something I'd love to try. His Instagram portal, Adam Ceramic, is full of encouraging, playful ways to get started with this technique.

- Keep on the path of self-discovery. I urge everyone, whatever their age, to jump into the fire and see what happens. You may get your fingers burned, but you'll also find beautiful new beginnings in the process.

10

KEEPING IT TOGETHER: OVER TO YOU

'We are in a process of becoming: it is not a place at which we arrive, although if we know the direction in which we are headed, we are more likely to thrive. To live a life that has meaning, a reason for being and a sense of belonging. A life in which we love and are loved.'

JULIA SAMUEL, *THIS TOO SHALL PASS*

Freya and I haven't seen each other for a while. Life, Covid mostly, has been in the way, but now the dust has settled, she's managed to make another winter getaway to stay with me in the Bahamas. I'm guilty of being solitary in my studio; on my own at my wheel, filling the kiln or fettling away listening to the radio. I love it. But I've missed Freya and working together. Last time we foraged and made a firepit on the beach; I wonder what we'll get up to with the tubs of glorious gloop I have at the back of my studio.

For the last two months, I have been preparing the clay we found with Doris Hamilton three years ago. I stirred and nurtured – probably even talked to it – every day as it matured into this rich, iron-heavy mud. Then I let it dry out on an old plaster board until it felt at its optimum wetness. When I first got my hands on it and kneaded it in preparation for throwing a few weeks ago, it felt perfect. A good 100kg is ready to go – around the same weight as a baby elephant. That's a lot of clay to play with.

The two of us have spoken briefly on the phone about what we want to achieve and make together. It feels extra exciting because an established gallery in Nassau has expressed an interest in showing our work. We're thrilled because any profits we make will go straight back to the sheltered workshop at the Beacon School in Freeport, Grand Bahama. This is where I met Doris and how I came to forage for the clay in the first place.

On the first day of her visit, Freya makes a beeline for the studio. Typically, when a potter knows there's clay nearby, it's like a bee to honey; they head straight for it. Even though she's around the stuff all the time, this is something else. She is doubly curious about the precious clay we found together. As soon as Freya starts kneading, the desire to go sunbathing and swimming disappears. I smile because I know that feeling well.

I encourage Freya to make herself at home at my wheel and she needs very little convincing. I sit opposite her on my teaching wheel, although now it's my time to learn again. We begin to throw. It's only really when we're sitting face to face, hands parallel, that the ebb and flow of our thoughts come to fruition. There's something about breathing in the same air, listening to our favourite music and touching our precious, foraged clay that brings us truly together.

There's a buzz of creative energy in the studio. The fluctuation of our thoughts as we build and sculpt together is tangible, yet the dynamic between us feels balanced and harmonious. Freya's strengths lie in building these big, elegant, feminine pots, while I'm more into pinching the clay into waves, petals and leaves. I watch intently as she builds big by throwing the pots in three or four parts. And I feel her eyes trained on what I'm doing too as I sculpt the rims of her beautifully thrown vases.

Then it's my turn to throw big. This is a process that involves throwing a pot in sections or parts, which then have to be pieced together by cross-hatching and using glue-like slip. The difficulty is in making the parts 'fit'; it requires both precision and a kind of wild confidence. I don't know why but I've shied away from piecing pottery together. There's too much that can go wrong: how do I make each piece centred? How do I attach the parts? What happens if everything falls apart in the kiln? Freya is a natural teacher who gently encourages me not to worry about making mistakes. 'What's the worst thing that can happen?' she laughs. 'There's heaps of clay; we just start again.'

Suddenly I'm off. I'm sticking long necks onto wide bellies and adding wide bellies to elegant feet. The key to building big, if you're going to make everything stick and stay together, is understanding the wetness of the clay. Your pieces will never attach if the clay is bone dry, which happens when you leave the clay too long. Equally, if you act too quickly, the clay will be too wet and the whole lot will collapse. Timing is crucial. The optimum moment to join your pieces is when the clay is leather hard. Start building from the base up, so that you make sure the piece is straight. Some find it helpful to use a spirit level for this. You also have to score the clay and crosshatch the surface of the joins deeper than you think; this technique acts like Velcro when the two pieces are finally joined. Then you need to dampen the rims of both pieces with a wet sponge until the clay feels sticky. You can now join them. The same technique is used for attaching handles.

'We should use the handles to make an entrance,' says Freya, as she carves off big hunks of clay. The large, statement handles she has in mind are a far cry from the functional, smaller ones I usually make. 'It should be like a catwalk,' she giggles. 'Let's really show off.' So we make these huge S-shaped, 6cm-wide handles, which look like enormous earrings when we stick them on the side of the jug. The pots really take on a life of their own. One jug appears to have a strong hand on its hip, poised to saunter down the runway. Another stands tall and proud and ready for anything. Meanwhile, I'm experiencing an epic rush of endorphins – in fact, it's a whole new kind of 'Hey, I feel like a professional'. I am no longer a frightened girl pinching away her fears but a fully fledged ceramicist working on her first show. Wahoo-whoosh. It hits me, body and soul.

———

It makes me laugh when I think back to meeting Freya's dad Chris Bramble all those years ago. I strolled into his studio and declared, 'I want to learn how to make a HUGE pot.' I'd only been practising for about a year so I was massively overstretching myself, but I'm good at masking nerves with overconfidence. I'm sure that all the seasoned potters in the room thought to themselves, 'Here's another one who thinks making an enormous pot on the wheel is child's play.' I was genuinely convinced that I could just hop on the wheel and it would take me a month or two to learn to throw big. But like most processes in pottery, it takes practice, and you make tons of mistakes before you create something good. So here I am, about seven years later, and I'm finally there.

After Freya went home from the 'big pot' trip, I was straight back at the wheel making more and more of these giant pots. They took months to complete and there was something rather special about them, so I lined up five of the best on the shoreline and snapped a photo of them. I love that no two pots are ever exactly the same, but there was a kind of uniform beauty to these confident vases as they stood tall before the setting sun.

I'll be forever grateful to Freya for sharing her knowledge and guiding me through the process. She will always be my teacher, but now she's become my collaborator too. This feels special because it happened so naturally. Neither of us planned the change in our relationship; it evolved gently from teaching into a friendship and from there it flowed into shared projects. Showing our work with the Cynthia Corbett Gallery at Miami Art Basel in December 2022 was a particular highlight. We both see this as a long-term collaboration and look forward to the exciting possibilities the future might bring.

Collaboration creates connection, and clay has a habit of making this happen. I mentioned the partnership between Picasso and Picault in Vallauris in the 1950s, and there have been many others through the ages. The artist Paul Gauguin experimented with sculptor and ceramicist Ernest Chaplet during the 1880s in Chaplet's Parisian studio. In this instance, Chaplet was the teacher, imparting his wide knowledge and understanding of clay, but they always shared the money they made from selling their wares. The partnership had started with Gauguin decorating the pots, but it wasn't long before he was making them too. Apparently, the collaboration was brief. They made around 50 stoneware pots together before Gauguin went his own way. He exchanged throwing on the wheel for hand building – coiling and slabbing mostly – to create around a hundred fantastical pieces of his own.

Fast forward to the 1940s and the partnership between Lucie Rie and Hans Coper, who had both settled in London after fleeing Nazi-occupied Europe (Rie from Austria and Coper from Germany). Rie was already an established potter when she set up her own studio in London in 1938. To start with, she made a living producing ceramic buttons for Harrods and Liberty's.

Some of these buttons were painstakingly created on the wheel, while others she made by hand or using moulds. Rie never lost her sense of fun – she gave her button ranges names like Star, Rose and Lettuce – but she took the art of button making very seriously, experimenting with both design (the simple twisted rope buttons are my favourites) and glazes. Nothing was too small for her artistic touch.

Rie later branched out into umbrella handles, brooches and mirror frames, but it was buttons that initially brought her and Coper together, when she employed him in 1946 to help fire them at her 'Button Factory'. Coper had no experience and had various health issues, including rheumatism, but he was eager to learn. Who knows what part clay had to play in his healing. It's incredible how quickly he got the hang of throwing pots – some say it only took a week – and by 1948 Rie and Coper were sharing a studio and exhibiting together.

It was a fruitful union, but in time they went their own ways, with Coper setting up his own studio in Hertfordshire. Rie is best known for her modernist forms, which somehow manage to balance functionality with invention and elegance. David Attenborough tells the story of buying one of Rie's beautiful coffee sets in the 1950s when he was setting up home with his wife. They were particularly taken with the pot, which had an unusual stick-like handle, and enjoyed using the entire set every day (as Rie intended), until a few cups were inevitably chipped and broken. Some time in the 1980s, the couple bought another set at auction: 'It had been made at roughly the same time as our first was and was very like it. The cost, alas, was seriously differ-ent.'[25] I know what he means; a few years ago I was lucky enough to buy just one of Rie's exquisite espresso cups at the Collect Art Fair at Somerset House and I'm quite sure David Attenborough would be even more shocked at how much that tiny cup cost me. I've sipped an espresso once from this cup and it tasted totally delicious, but most of the time it's safely stowed away.

These days, owning a Hans Coper is a dream that's totally out of my reach. Some of his sculptural pieces are huge – those 7-foot candlesticks in Coventry Cathedral, for example, are awesome – and sadly out of budget. In 2018, one of his vases set a new record for a piece of British studio pottery, when it fetched over six figures at auction. The stoneware vase had cost £250 in the 1970s but the seller had stashed it in a shoebox for years because she thought it was ugly. I love these 'cash in the attic' stories but I'm also happy Coper is respected and collected globally. 'I am a potter,' Rie said of her old friend, 'but he was an artist.' Her modesty shines through and I wonder whether he would have discovered his genius without their friendship. Clay became his ultimate means of expression, but would he have found it without Rie to guide and support him?

Recently, I have embarked on a new collaboration of my own, with jewellery designer Monica Vinader. Monica set out to create a line of jewellery that women would want to buy for themselves at a price they could afford – beautiful rings and trinkets that felt individual and luxurious yet are made from recycled gold and silver with ethically sourced stones.

Monica and I started out as friends and then in early 2020 she talked about branching out into homeware and asked whether I'd like to help. I loved the idea, imagining I could make a pot here and a pot there, but Monica made it very clear that this wasn't what she meant – she was looking for large-scale production. By chance, a few months earlier, I'd been in talks with a company who could help oversee production of my wares in Portugal. The idea of building a collection with Monica was very appealing and now a potential reality.

Literally a month later, the world was in lockdown and our plans were put on hold. Part of me felt relieved. At that point it felt just too soon and I'm not sure I would have coped under the pressure. However, about a year later, Monica reached out to me again. I'd been cooped up for months – we all had – and being part of the real world again was a frightening proposition. But luckily something inside me had changed. I was no less scared but I was open to new possibilities – maybe clay had done the trick? Either way, I felt safe in Monica's hands. Monica and I share a love of Bahamian sandy beaches, turquoise seas and postcard sunsets, so we kicked off our collaborative designs with a set of three stacking dishes with whispers of glimmering gold on the edges in shades that encapsulate the skies, the setting sun and the beautiful sea. The idea was to make delicate dishes, perfect for stashing jewellery or other bits and bobs.

I'm really proud of our first collaboration. It's totally different from my projects with Freya, in which we make one-off pieces to showcase in galleries. With Monica it's large-scale manufacturing. As always, the process begins in my studio where I design and make the prototype. I then hand the sample over to a factory in Portugal where the pieces are reproduced in bulk using the slip cast method. At the time of writing this, I'm creating a bud vase with Monica. It looks simple, but it's delicate and deceptively tricky to get just right. The artist Constantin Brancusi is our inspiration – a Romanian genius who worked in the 1930s carving abstract sculptures of birds and heads in stone and then casting them in bronze. You can see where my fingers have pressed into the clay, so that despite being set in a mould and produced on a large scale, the personal touch will be there to behold.

Women have to go that extra mile to prove themselves and Monica has done that by building a brilliant group of people around her. This is another form of collaboration and I'm lucky to be able to watch and learn from an experienced businesswoman who believes in teamwork. However strong your team is, I've discovered that setting up a business can be tough. Production in the Portuguese factories has been very stop and start. I've sometimes worried that this isn't my thing; I can take a ball of clay and have a finished pot within weeks, whereas mass production seems to take months. I'm gradually getting my head around these different processes and just learning as I go.

*

Although building BIG is wonderfully compelling, making something small can be just as satisfying. I used various ways to keep my head together during lockdown, but making buttons was a real saviour. Pinching clay soothed me during this tricky time when I was mostly away from my studio as Jimmy recovered from pneumonia and the island was slowly getting back to normal after the turmoil of Hurricane Matthew.

If you're new to clay, this is an easy thing to try at home. You can start with a small ball of kneaded clay in your hand and gently mould it into your button shape. Or you can begin with a larger ball of clay and roll it out like pastry, then cut out a variety of shapes – hearts, squares or hexagons, for example – with the help of a cookie cutter. From there you can experiment with decoration. While the clay is still wet, make two holes with a needle. Some potters fire the buttons to bisque and use a small drill to pierce the holes, but I prefer doing this by hand to avoid accidental cracks. I tend to glaze my buttons on one side as it's less fiddly to then fire and I love to see the raw clay on the base of each one. You can also thread the buttons onto special wire and glaze both sides, or use props.

Buttons are a real labour of love and they make wonderful

gifts. Being hand-made, they have that extra-special, personal touch. You don't always need a kiln; you can use air-dry clay or polymer clay, Fimo, instead. There are lots of button-making tutorials on YouTube if you need inspiration. It's also a great project if you want to get your children involved. They will more than likely go free-range and find their own rules for making them. Children are brilliant at that. If all else fails, you can make some beads together.

Another coping method I discovered during lockdown was inspired by the polyvagal theory – I say 'inspired' because I took just the bits I found helpful and tried to apply them to my life. The vagus nerve is the longest nerve in the body, connecting your brain to many important organs, including the gut, heart and lungs. The vagus nerve has many jobs but what I'm most fascinated by is how it affects the parasympathetic nervous system. Once triggered, the parasympathetic side helps to create calm by bringing down your blood pressure and heart rate and making you feel safe. This was something that interested me, particularly during the pandemic, when I felt scared and worried for my family – especially for Jimmy after his pneumonia.

So how do we increase our vagal response? Acute cold exposure is one way. Cold water swimming has become much more popular recently because of the buzz and feeling of wellbeing it offers, but apparently just submerging your face is enough to stimulate the vagus nerve. Deep and slow breathing is another way to stimulate it – also singing and chanting, taking probiotics for gut health, meditation and exercise.

Throughout my life, when things have become angsty, I've always tended to run from the source of apprehension – I'm classic Mrs Flight over Fight – but just a little knowledge about the vagus nerve now helps me to check in and calm my mind. If the children are squabbling or I'm just feeling overwhelmed, I try to step away for a moment so I can properly assess where my nervous system is at. I go through a few questions in my head like: am I in my head or am I in my heart? Do I want to run? Am I breathing properly? Once I can put a label on how I'm feeling, I begin to calm down. Add in some breath work and I'm able to resume normal service. This is probably a very simplistic version of the theory, but it works for me. Kneading clay has a similar effect at calming my nerves, however, I can't always get my hands on it. I'm learning to name and understand what's going on in my body instead and I've discovered it's quite effective.

Children have much to teach us on this score: they don't need to check in with themselves, or name their feelings. They just *are*. I was reminded of this by something that happened with Jimmy not long ago. He has always loved being around clay, and on afternoons in my studio is more than happy just sticking his hands into the bin of recycled clay; sinking his fingers deep into the mud, enjoying the messy, silky-soft earth in his palms. I usually let him get on with this, but one day I thought it was time for him to take a step up.

'Okay Jim, we're not going to play with that today,' I said. He looked a little disappointed. 'We're going to make a pot on the wheel.' Instantly, his face lit up. Great, I thought; we're in this together.

I began to go through the process with him, and before I knew it we were off. The wheel was spinning, and his hands were cupping the clay as I poured water from a sponge onto his fingers. 'Right now, Jimmy,' I said, 'take your thumbs and dig them deep into the centre of the clay.'

His thumbs began to push – slowly and steadily – he is a natural. But just a matter of seconds later, the wheel stopped abruptly. 'No, Mama. I want to make a mountain.'

I paused, choosing my words. 'Okay, Jim, but how much did you love Iris's pot that she made?' I didn't want to give up on my plan for him. He considered this, shrugged his shoulders and we pressed on, my hand on the pedal of the wheel again. As the wheel sped up he pressed his thumbs in deeper, but I sensed his anguish and we soon stopped again.

Jim was cross. He didn't want a mountain with a hole in it. 'You'll feel so pleased with yourself when you've made it, Jimmy,'

I said. 'You can put your special Lego in it. We can pour water from it. A little flower can live in it or maybe it can be a home for a beetle.' But my attempts at selling the notion of a vessel to a four-year-old were in vain. He was fuming. He slapped the clay hard. Not just a tap but a thud that sounded like a tennis ball hitting deep in the middle of a racket.

'Stop!' I was so ready to reproach him, desperate to offload my wisdom, share my preconceived notions of what was right and what made sense in my mind. And yet, in that split second, I became acutely aware of his wisdom. He needed the mountain. The beauty of its simplicity was tangible. With the vibration from that intensely fierce slap against the wet clay still lingering in the air, we looked at each other and started laughing.

This is what it's all about... I learned more from Jimmy in that moment than I could ever teach him and I was reminded of Picasso's words, 'It took me four years to paint like Raphael and a lifetime to paint like a child.' Picasso came into pottery relatively later in life, but within a short amount of time created thousands of ceramic designs, many of which had this playful, unsophisticated decoration. I don't think anyone could have told him what to do and he created whatever he felt like.

And this is my message to you. Explore what makes you feel better, and when you work out what it is then just keep doing it. As well as writing inspiring books, Julia Samuel is a soothing presence on Instagram; her words of wisdom and tools for living are like balm for an uneasy mind. In Stress Awareness Month in 2022 (this happens every April) she reminded us that creativity is a way of tackling depression, anxiety and burn-out. By taking your mind and thinking to a creative place, you form new images, thoughts and space, which calm and nourish the soul. She urges us to look to music, art and poetry to find inner peace.

Fully immerse yourself in this idea and get involved in making and experimenting with whatever appeals to you, whether that be music, art, writing or baking bread. Pauline Beaumont got me thinking about this with her book *Bread Therapy: The Mindful Art of Baking Bread.*[26] As soon as she mentioned the parallel between bread making and pottery I was there. She understands how the kneading actions involved in both engages the same parts of our bodies and brains. And she knows all too well that twitchy-itchy-excited waiting game you play while your pots are in the kiln because she feels that same edgy expectation as her bread bakes in the oven. 'Like becoming a potter, to become a breadmaker is to become a craftsperson,' writes Pauline. 'It is something that will enrich your life as well as your larder and can become part of your identity – part of who you are as well as what you do.'

Baking bread isn't pottery but it's a sister act. It still gives me the buzz I need because I'm artistically engaged. The very act of kneading the dough relaxes me. I also love decorating the baked loaves; out comes my beloved sgraffito tool and I scrape pictures into the flour that I've sprinkled on top. Sometimes I scatter flowers and herbs over the crusty surface, and somehow these flourishes make the bread look more delicious. There has even been a touch of Picasso in some of the drawings I've made, so I call them my 'Picassourdough'. Again, creativity is the key to easing my anxiety. I truly believe that finding my creative self has helped me to stay antidepressant-free.

Disclaimer: I'm not a doctor. I'm thankful for how Prozac has helped me and I've witnessed first-hand how antidepressants have benefitted so many other people through difficult times. However, I don't think there's enough support for people when they want to stop taking the tablets. Doctors prescribe antidepressants so easily, yet they don't provide a service to help us come off them. Clay helped me to gently move away from relying on them – and I was given the right professional help and family support to cushion my weaning-off process. It might be something very different for you, but hopefully my story shows that there is always a way forward.

As ever in life, it's helpful to be reminded that learning is ongoing and so is change. For me, the secrets of clay just keep spilling forth. Nowadays, I can tell instantly how wet an unfired pot is just by touching the rim with my lips. Likewise, I can

gauge whether a pot is bisque or fired to full temperature by putting my tongue on it – if it's bisque, your tongue kind of sticks to it like a prawn cracker. I have a kind of intuition and knowledge that I believe will only increase with time, so it feels like I've completed my first lap on this particular course.

Going back to Picasso and this idea of learning the rules so you can break them, I think I've hit that moment too, so on my next lap I'm going even further into the art of pottery with a detour into geology to further my understanding of glaze making and where all this stuff actually comes from. When I look at my original pieces, they're a far cry from what I'm creating now.

Back then, I really knew what I wanted to produce, but I didn't have all the skills. I would try to be abstract, but I didn't necessarily have the foundations.

Many of the greatest artists only began to play with the process after years of studying or suffering for their art. Jackson Pollock was a struggling alcoholic when he began experimenting with pouring and dripping paint onto the canvas. People have tried to emulate his splatter art for decorative effect, but somehow the passion, rage or unpredictability is missing. Vincent Van Gogh is another artist who makes it look easy, but he practised for years before painting his profoundly sad and moving *Starry Night*. Lucio Fontana was a religious portrait painter before he slashed his plain canvases. We've all heard the kind of criticism these artworks get, 'Surely anyone could cut a canvas like that?' Now I know more about him, I think I understand the beauty of Fontana's work and the skill involved. Those slashes are filled with an intention and expression that maybe wouldn't be there if he hadn't understood the rules of classical art first.

As a beginner, my process was gung-ho, but I made some beautiful pieces, too. My fragile porcelain shell that cracked in the kiln was one of my favourites. Back then, if I wanted to make a globe I'd use a mould, but these days I know how to make one on the wheel. My evolving understanding of the medium means that I have more choices available to me. I'm still proud of my early abstract sculptures and plan to revisit some of those forms one day. I don't know whether Barbara Hepworth felt the same way, but she often returned to similar shapes and ideas. I wonder whether this is because she wanted to improve on previous pieces or simply continue experimenting. Is this what growing wiser and being open to change means? Sometimes change is forced upon us, but I do believe that it brings with it the opportunity for growth and happiness. By taking things slowly and steadily – one step at a time – a happy future can lie ahead.

'If you hear a voice within saying 'you cannot paint,' then by all means, paint,' wrote Van Gogh, 'and that voice will be silenced.' Once upon a time I took a ball of clay and rolled with it. Somehow all those voices – 'the shitty committee' – in my head were silenced and I found a happiness I didn't expect to discover there. I've told my tale about depression, my need to knead and how pottery heals me. I started with a pinch pot. My son Jimmy made a mountain. Now it's your turn. What are you going to try?

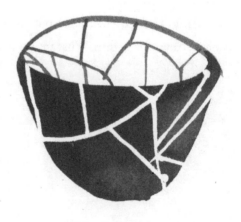

FLEA BITES

- How many people look back on their lives and wonder why they didn't see the right path a little sooner into their journey? There's no rush to get to where you're going. I try to enjoy the scenery and never stop looking for what makes me happy.

- As Carl Jung said, 'The privilege of a lifetime is to become who you truly are.' We are always a work in progress.

- Never forget the art of watching others in action. If you can't be in the studio, you can tune in online. I recommend following Miami-based Key West Pottery for inspiration on throwing large and joining those parts together.

- There's a wonderful saying: 'if you want something done, ask a busy person'. I say ask a potter. They are experts at spinning plates and juggling pottery processes; cleaning, teaching, chatting and chattering all at the same time. And once you've become a dab hand in the studio, you can learn to do it in life. You can be a businessperson, parent, friend, creative – the whole lot if you like.

- Nick Cave confirms many of my own feelings about the healing powers of clay in his book *Faith, Hope and Carnage*. In his words : 'There is something very elemental about working with clay that draws you in and takes over, calms you. I got lost in it. It was exactly what I needed at the time... The action of pushing my fingers into this elemental stuff had a kind of trancelike effect that delivered me to some other place- sort of part childhood, part outer space... it felt liberating and also very healing'.

- Keep experimenting, playing, pushing the clay to its limits and most importantly, have a laugh doing it.

- Over to you...

ACKNOWLEDGMENTS

'Pottery has its own language and inherent laws, and words have theirs, and neither can be bound by the other. Nevertheless a certain amount of translation and interpretation is possible provided a potter can find the words, or a writer insight into pottery.'

BERNARD LEACH, *A POTTER'S BOOK*

Thank you to my friend Liz Flavell, an editor, writer, poet, mother, music fanatic and fellow sea lover. Her empathy, calm nature and poetic way has allowed for a creative collaborative fizz or WHOOOOSH that felt completely right from the moment we met in lockdown virtually. One of the best bits about getting older is making new friends, and despite being oceans apart, I have made a friend for life. Over to Liz: 'Clay has this way of bringing people together and so do words. Funnily enough, we found that creating pots is not so far removed from writing books. It can take a while for things to take shape (or moments on a wheel) and inevitably you have to shave away layers to reveal the true beauty. Then come the flourishes and finishing touches – you love a sgraffito pen as much as I adore a metaphor. Sometimes things don't go to plan but that's when the magic happens.'

Thank you to Rupert 'reflexologist' for helping me to 'get the baby out', for introducing me to your partner Rebecca Cripps. Rebecca, your positivity and advice at the beginning of lockdown gave me that confidence boost I needed to take this idea to the next stage. The stars were aligned and I met the fantastic, hand-holding, morale-boosting Gordon Wise, in whose hands I immediately felt safe. Thank you, Gordon, and your wonderful team at Curtis Brown.

Thank you to Vanessa Beaumont. Thanks to Aurea Carpenter and Rebecca Nicolson for jumping at this project. From Short Books to Octopus the transition was seamless. Thanks to the wonderful Helena Sutcliffe – you are a magical editor with the brightest future. Thank you for letting me be a part of your own adventure and to Jo Copestick, Meg Brown, Mel Four, Lara Harwood, Sue Amaradivakara and Katherine Stroud.

Thank you, Chris Bramble for your generosity. It's essential that ancestral skills like yours should be passed on – you do this with such grace. To your girls Yolanda and Freya… long may the magic last. To all at Kingsgate Workshops and Kindred Studios – it takes a village. Thank you Gregory Tingay, Mary Reynolds and to my sister Alice BB for your time and editing.

Thank you, Emmy and Simone. Thank you, mama Nancy, for being my rock. Thanks to Dario, Wendy, Tiffany, Sharon and to all my island friends who have been a support. To Grand Bahama – from within your isolation I experienced my fertile void and found the solace I needed to get creative and heal. Thank you, Doris Hamilton, Mrs Colebrooke and the Beacon School. Thank you, Monica Vinader and all your hardworking team. Thank you to the Tern gallery, Cynthia Corbett gallery, Studio Pottery London, the Sladmore Gallery.

Thank you, Lauren, Klara, Olivia and Mary.

Thank you to Julia, Leon, Isabel, Miles and Luiza. 'Therapy works'.

Thank you, Vixen, for your unwavering friendship.

To the PICU ward at St. Mary's Paddington and Dr. Simon Nadel for saving Jimmy's life and to his guardian angel Maura – our lives would not be the same without you.

Thanks to Granny Hen for your energy, love and support, to Sarah and Fati for the swims and giggles and to all the extended StGs – I feel very lucky being married into this beautiful family.

Poops, Hen and Babbly for tolerating your runt.

Mama and Papa – for giving me everything plus that little bit more.

To my Pin, I love you more than I did yesterday and less than I will tomorrow. Here's to the next ten years of marriage.

To my Shrimp and Jim-Jam, this book is dedicated to all three of you.

FURTHER READING

I've found inspiration for making pots and creating a better life from many sources. Books, articles and podcasts have helped me find my path to healing. Here are just some of the many sources of wisdom I've discovered along the way:

Mad, Bad and Sad – Lisa Appignanesi
The Heart of Mindful Relationships – Maria Arpa
The Antidepressant Fact Book – Peter R. Breggin, M.D.
*Daring Greatly: How the Courage to be Vulnerable Trans-
    forms the Way We Live, Love, Parent and Lead* – Brené
    Brown
12 Birds to Save Your Life, Nature's Lessons in Happiness –
    Charlie Corbett
Mental Healing Through Clay – Elisa Dalle Molle
Be Your Own CBT Therapist – Windy Dryden
The Choice – Edith Eger
Man's Search for Meaning – Victor Frankl
*The Potter's Dictionary of Material and Techniques,
    Sixth Edition* – Frank Hamer and Janet Hamer

Lost Connections: Why You're Depressed and How to Find Hope – Johann Hari

Period Power – Maisie Hill

Mindfulness for Mums – Izzy Judd

The Art of Creative Thinking – Rod Judkins

Calm the F**k Down – Sarah Knight

The Life-Changing Magic of Not Giving a F**k – Sarah Knight

The Clay Cure, Natural Healing from the Earth – Ran Knishinsky

The Pottery Handbook – Simon Leach

H is for Hawk – Helen Macdonald

Jog On – Bella Mackie

The Wise Earth Speaks to Your Spirit – Janell Moon

The Pottery Studio Handbook – Kristin Muller

Where the Crawdads Sing – Delia Owens

The Book You Wish Your Parents Had Read – Phillipa Perry

Reclaiming the Wild Soul – Mary Reynolds Thompson

Smile: The Story of a Face – Sarah Ruhl

The Potter's Bible – Marilyn Scott

Hand Built – Melissa Weiss

Freud on Women – Elisabeth Young-Bruehl

REFERENCES

1. 'Prioritizing these three things will improve your life – and maybe even save it', Colby Itkowitz, *The Washington Post*, 28 April 2017, https://www.washingtonpost.com/news/inspired-life/wp/2017/04/28/prioritizing-these-three-things-will-improve-your-life-and-maybe-even-save-it/

2. 'Throws of passion: how pottery became a refuge from our hyperconnected times', Richard Godwin, *The Guardian*, 25 August 2019, https://www.theguardian.com/artanddesign/2019/aug/25/throws-of-passion-how-pottery-became-a-refuge-from-our-hyperconnected-times

3. *This Too Shall Pass: Stories of Change, Crises and Hopeful Beginnings*, Julia Samuel (Penguin, 2020); '5 steps to mental well being', NHS website, https://www.nhs.uk/mental-health/self-help/guides-tools-and-activities/five-steps-to-mental-wellbeing/#:~:text=Research%20shows%20that%20learning%20new,you%20to%20connect%20with%20others

4. *Thrown*, Sara Cox (Coronet, 2022)

5. 'How we made the Tower of London poppies', Imogen Tilden, *The Guardian*, 5 March 2018, https://www.theguardian.com/artanddesign/2018/mar/05/how-we-made-tower-of-london-poppies-paul-cummins-tom-piper

6. *The Scent of Dried Roses*, Tim Lott (Penguin, 2009)

7. *Touching Clay, Touching What? The Use of Clay in Therapy*, Lynne Souter-Anderson (Archive Publishing, 2010)

8. *Barbara Hepworth: Art & Life*, Eleanor Clayton and Ali Smith (Thames and Hudson, 2021)

9. Gestalt therapy is a type of psychotherapy that encourages individuals to become more aware of their thoughts, feelings, and behaviours in the present moment, and to take responsibility for their own experiences and actions. The goal of gestalt therapy is to

help individuals gain insight and self-awareness, develop a greater sense of authenticity and wholeness, and improve their relationships with others: https://gestaltcentre.org.uk/what-is-gestalt/

10. *The Whole-Brain Child*, Dr. Daniel J. Siegel and Dr. Tina Payne Bryson (Hachette, 2019)

11. *Lifting Depression: a Neuroscientist's Hands-On Approach to Activating Your Brain's Healing Power*, Dr. Kelly Lambert (Basic Books, 2010)

12. *Beyond East and West: Memoirs, Portraits and Essays*, Bernard Leach (Faber & Faber, 2012)

13. Why we shouldn't be scrutinising Seth Rogen's ceramics, Casey Lesser, Artsy.net, 14 June 2019, https://www.artsy.net/article/artsy-editorial-scrutinizing-seth-rogens-ceramics

14. https://www.nct.org.uk/life-parent/how-you-might-be-feeling/your-experiences-having-another-baby-after-pnd

15. https://www.ecdc.europa.eu/en/news-events/rsv-virus-expected-add-pressure-hospitals-many-eueea-countries-season

16. Isaac Button, Country Potter (extract), https://www.youtube.com/watch?v=l4qdGTFBRJ4

17. *Beyond East and West: Memoirs, Portraits and Essays*, Bernard Leach (Faber & Faber, 2012)

18. Janet Haig, Siberia Saved Me, https://www.youtube.com/watch?v=EmlsqIUqXHo

19. https://wepresent.wetransfer.com/stories/nigel-slater-ceramics

20. *Boy in a China Shop*, Keith Brymer Jones (Hodder & Stoughton, 2022)

21. *Alternative Kilns and Firing Techniques*, James C. Watkins and Paul Andrew Wandless (2007)

22. *Reasons to Stay Alive*, Matt Haig (Canongate, 2015)

23. *Everyday Sacred: A Woman's Journey Home*, Sue Bender (Harper San Fransisco, 1995)

24. *The Prophet*, Khalil Gibran (Wisehouse Classics Edition, 2020)

25. Sir David Attenborough remembers Dame Lucie Rie, Sothebys.com, 5 September 2017, https://www.sothebys.com/en/articles/sir-david-attenborough-remembers-dame-lucie-rie

26. *Bread Therapy: The Mindful Art of Baking Bread*, Pauline Beaumont (Yellow Kite, 2020)

ABOUT THE AUTHOR

Florence St. George, also known as Flea, is a British ceramicist who discovered her love of clay after the birth of her daughter when she became ill with postnatal depression. In 2020, Flea became a contestant on *The Great Pottery Throw Down*. On the show she revealed her unique style, and achieved the ultimate *Throw Down* compliment when she brought a tear to the eye of judge Keith Brymer-Jones. She has recently collaborated with the jeweller Monica Vinader. Inspired by the power of pottery and its healing, meditative abilities, Florence feels happiest in her studio. She lives in the UK with her husband and two children.

Website: www.florencestgeorge.com
Instagram: @florencestgeorge